The Memory Exchange

By: Mustafa Nejem

PROLOGUE

"The Memory Exchange" In NeoMind, where memories are the currency, Leah, an artist drowning in debt, stumbles upon an underground market where the most cherished moments are sold for financial gains. As she delves into this dark labyrinth, she uncovers a disturbing secret about the origin of these memories and the heart-wrenching repercussions they have on those who trade them. This discovery triggers a frantic quest for truth, leading her to challenge the confines of the city and confront the deepest, most sinister secrets of this nostalgia-driven economy.

.

CONTENTS

Chapter 1

A World of Memories

The first rays of the sun peeked timidly through the tall buildings of NeoMind, as if they were painting every corner of the city with light. The skyscrapers, tall and gleaming, looked like metal giants that held stories around every corner. Leah, almost like a whisper in the darkness, moved carefully through the shadows that stretched across the streets. Her footsteps, light but firm, echoed on the pavement like small heartbeats in the midst of the stillness.

The streets were filled with a kind of silent magic. There, between the buildings, memories floated, as if the air were filled with tales of yesteryear. The sounds of laughter from other times were interspersed with choked sighs and tears that no one remembered anymore. It was like walking on an invisible river, where past feelings flowed unnoticed, a torrent of emotions mixing in a secret dance. Leah, with curious eyes, was entering this world of stored sensations. Every step she took seemed to awaken a different echo, a different murmur in the symphony of memories that filled the air. All around her, the walls seemed to be mute witnesses of all these experiences. The tall buildings were like open books, full of stories waiting to be discovered by those who dared to pay attention to them.

On the loom of NeoMind, Leah continued her walk, weaving her existence among the melodies of memory. Every forgotten smile and faded tear was intertwined with its own story. It was part of the city's symphony, one more note in the concert of memories that danced in its streets. With each step, she plunged into the unfathomable river of memories, being both a spectator and a protagonist of the lives that lurked in the shadows, being part of the very life that flowed through the alleys and squares of the city.

At the heart of NeoMind, Leah harbored artistic yearnings as she delved into a city of dreams and ambitions. The city was not reduced to gleaming skyscrapers; It was a vast melting pot where memories were displayed as treasures, like coins in the air, prized goods for which everyone craved. It was a place that moved to the rhythm of longing for the past and the desire to treasure what had been lived. Here, every corner vibrated with nostalgia for yesterday and the fervent desire to preserve what was already gone.

NeoMind wasn't just a site, it was a vast backdrop where memories sparkled like priceless gems. People exhibited them, exchanged them, coveted them as if they were tokens in a game where everyone aspired to be the victors. The city was nourished and animated by these memories, as if they were the very heartbeat of life that flowed through its streets. Memories were the constant throbbing that fueled every corner of NeoMind, like an engine that propelled its existence.

NeoMind's economy was like a whirlwind of feelings clinging to the past. Everyone was immersed in a sea of emotions that came and went like the waves of the sea. Nostalgia, that melancholy for what once was, echoed in every corner, reminding everyone of what was once important. The fervent desire to retain what had already slipped through their fingers kept people in an eternal attempt to hold time, as if they wanted to capture the moments with their own hands and prevent them from vanishing into thin air. It was a

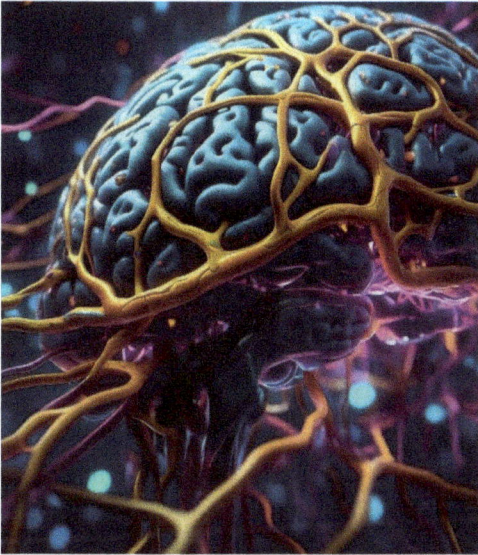

constant dance between wanting to hold on to memories and at the same time letting them flow, as if each transaction was an attempt to stop the clock and preserve the essence of what was fading.

NeoMind was like a giant canvas where every brushstroke of the past intermingled with present desires. Leah saw the city as a creative challenge, a stage where she longed for her art to shine among the flashes of memories and longings.

She dreamed of weaving her works into that infinite symphony of experiences that the city jealously guarded. However, she understood that in this world where the past was so treasured, standing out was a challenge, as her art could be diluted in the dense fog of nostalgia and ambition for what was already gone. For her, finding a way for her art to shine through that gale of memories would be a momentous challenge.

For Leah, art was like breathing, like speaking in a noisy place. It was her way of expressing what she felt, of telling her story without the need for words.

But while art filled her life with meaning, it couldn't solve those money problems that had her worried. Her paintings were like a diary of her imagination, full of colors and shapes that told what she had inside, but in this city, that wasn't enough.

Leah's canvases were like windows to her inner world, each stroke a melody of her emotions turned into colors and shapes. Each work was like a living chapter of her own story, a palpable reflection of her creative soul. But in this corner where nostalgia had more value than the present itself, Leah's art seemed to be shipwrecked in the ocean of longings of the past. Despite the richness of her works, in this setting where memories were traded, her art struggled to stand out from the brilliance of what it once was.

Although for her, each work was like a little piece of her being captured in colors, in NeoMind only memories had that value with which she could negotiate.

It was as if people were willing to spend a lot to relive a moment that had already passed, but not so much for something new, for something that someone else was creating in the present. And for Leah, that situation was like fighting against a very strong current, where her creations sometimes seemed to be shipwrecked in a sea of memories cherished by others.

Leah walked through the crowded markets, where holograms shone everywhere, like colored lights telling stories. The ads glowed, inviting her to buy those encapsulated memories. She saw people, with eager eyes, holding devices like treasures, as if those devices were magical portals to times long gone. Some were smiling, others seemed lost in their own thoughts, all immersed in buying and selling experiences. It was like walking through a festival of colors and sparkles that showed fragments of lives

People held these devices with reverence, as if they were buried treasures that they dug up to complete their own story. There were those who looked longing, their eyes shining as they relived moments that had been left behind in time. Others sought to acquire other people's memories, as if they were pieces of a puzzle, wishing to fill in the gaps in their own stories.

Leah was immersed in this whirlwind of intertwined emotions. She watched as people clung to these devices with poignant intensity, as if each hologram were a treasure chest, enclosing laughter, tears, and hugs suspended in time. Each hologram seemed to be a glimpse of encapsulated life, an echo of what was and no longer is, or what never came to be but someone

fervently longed for. To many, they were like tiny relics, pieces of their own history or an imagined world, jealously guarded as priceless treasures.

Amid the multitude of stares lost in holographic screens, Leah was both curious and bewildered. For her, art was the living manifestation of the present, a reflection of what she felt at the time, but for many there, it seemed that the past was the most valuable. And in the midst of that hubbub, as she watched as everyone searched for their own piece of history in those shiny machines, she wondered where her art fit into a world that traded in past memories.

In the hustle and bustle of that crowd immersed in her own reminiscences, Leah felt like an island in a choppy ocean. Despite being surrounded by faces and figures, she found herself isolated in her own universe, as if her own memories were slowly fading in the overwhelming glow of other people's memories. It was as if her inner world, full of experiences and emotions, was dwarfed by the overwhelming torrent of memories floating in the public sphere.

It was as if every laugh, every tear she had experienced, became blurred in the tangle of other people's memories that filled the air. She longed to find her place in that world where people valued those little pieces of their history so much, where memories were more than just photos of the past, they were coins that were exchanged daily.

For Leah, her art was like the open book of her personal history, a canvas on which she painted her feelings and emotions. However, in this place, it seemed that her artistic expression was not as appreciated as those digital images that captivated everyone. It was as if her voice was immersed in the din of the glittering screens, which showcased the most intimate and poignant moments of others, while her own narrative faded among the wave of other people's memories.

Within this whirlwind of memories, each one valued and sought after like precious treasures, Leah's art appeared to fade away, akin to a shooting star amidst a sky aglow with artificial lights. Despite her earnest yearning to carve her niche in this realm of memories, she felt like an outsider in a space where the worth of personal expression was overshadowed by the insatiable desires of others.

NeoMind, a city where the vibrant lights waltzed gracefully with the enigmatic shadows, presented itself to Leah as an expansive canvas bursting with enigmas and paradoxes. It seemed as though every street traversed was a distinct stroke on a vast canvas, and each towering building a vibrant hue in a palette that intermingled to form an immense yet intricate masterpiece. There existed a certain allure in its diversity, a captivating beauty that fascinated her, yet it was accompanied by a complexity so intricate that it eluded complete understanding.

In a world where memories shone like stars in the sky, Leah longed to transcend mere existence. She

was looking for more than just surviving among so many memories. She longed to discover a meaning, a purpose that would give meaning to her art. In the midst of that maelstrom of emotions floating in the air, she longed to find a space where her creations weren't just another voice among the noise. She wanted her art to be a melody capable of resonating deeply in the hearts of those who appreciated it, like a guiding beacon through the mist.

However, that search confronted her with difficult crossroads. The art that pulsed inside her was awsome, her way of communicating with the world, but at NeoMind, where memories were bought and sold as if they were humanity's last breath, the need to survive clashed with her desire to create.

Every day was a struggle between the urge to follow her passion and the pressure to adapt to a city that seemed to turn its back on the very essence of what she loved to do.

Leah stops at that crossroads, and before her eyes an impressive spectacle unfolds. It's like an endless dance of people buying and selling souvenirs, as if they were precious treasures exchanged in a market. Holograms sparkle, showing moments that were once intimate and are now displayed to the public as if they were merchandise. As she watches this scene, she feels as if her own essence is vanishing among all those other people's experiences. It's as if her identity is diluted in a sea of memories that don't belong to her, a tide that threatens to take her own memories with her.In that instant, something changes inside Leah. An impregnable force rises within her.

An iron determination is forged in her heart. She decides that, no matter the difficulties, she will find her place in that world of memories. Even if that means going into the darkest and most unknown corners of NeoMind, she is willing to explore those places where few dare to venture. She is ready to dive into the depths of her own thoughts and emotions, ready to discover her true self in the midst of an environment that seemed to want to rob her identity.

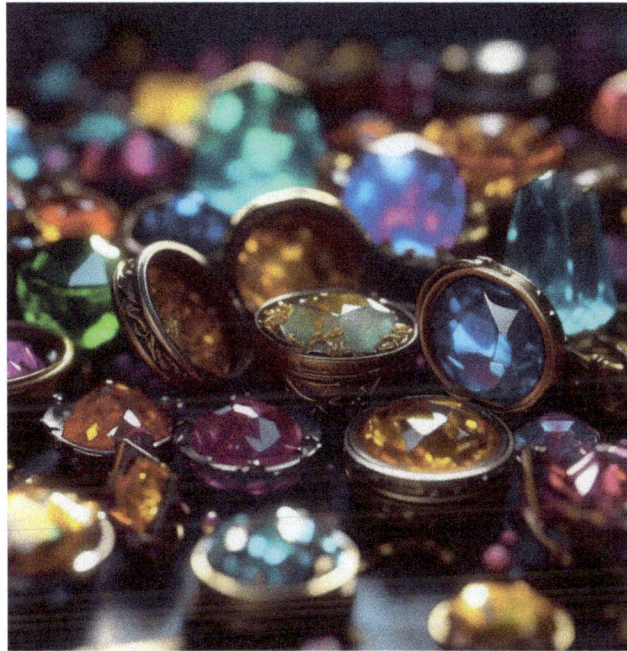

Chapter 2

The Revelation of the
Underground Market

In the shadows of NeoMind, as the sunlight gave way to darkness, mysterious melodies emerged from every corner. The city came alive with an evening concert, where each singular sound told its own story. Holograms, like futuristic fireflies, flashed colors in the corners, creating a ballet of lights in the gloom. Between confidential whispers and secret transactions, an urban symphony was woven that flooded the air, a unique composition that characterized the nights in this enigmatic place.

On that particular night, a cold breeze filtered through the narrow alleys, carrying with it an air of change. It was as if the wind was trying to push Leah toward an encounter that was destined to change the course of her life. The whispers of the wind seemed to carry coded messages, mysterious signals that impelled her to follow the path marked by that icy gust.

It was as if the universe was conspiring to lead her to a destination she did not yet know, but which was about to unfold before her eyes.Leah was walking down a little-traveled street, where the usual bustle seemed to have faded, leaving only a few hurried passers-by. In that haven of stillness, something suddenly caught her eye. A sudden flash caught her gaze, as if a rainbow were escaping from a half-open door. The vivid and radiant colors shone, standing out among the monotony of city lights, creating a hypnotic contrast in the gloom.

Curiosity ignited in her chest, like a spark that stoked her artistic spirit. It was as if that door hid a canvas to be discovered, an unknown work of art that called to her strongly. The temptation of the unknown caressed her mind, leading her to make an impulsive decision.

Without a second thought, she ventured toward the mysterious threshold, leaving behind the safety of the known to plunge into the enigmatic and unknown.

With careful steps, Leah walked through the entrance, entering a scenario that defied her imagination. Before her unfolded an underground market, a hidden universe manifesting itself in the shadows, a sanctum in darkness where the murmurs of under-the-rope transactions competed with the glow of devices full of memories. It was as if she had entered a parallel world, where the forbidden and the coveted intertwined in a subtle dance.

The scene was captivating: the crowd moved in theatrical silence, as if they were dancing to the beat

of a shared secret. Barely audible whispers wafted through the air, mingling with flashing lights that reflected on the expectant faces of those who entered the clandestine compound.

Every gesture, every exchange, was shrouded in mystery, as if each object changed hands, carrying with it an encrypted history that only a privileged few could decipher. Leah felt like a privileged spectator, a witness to an intriguing spectacle. The atmosphere resonated with a unique energy, a mixture of excitement and danger that was palpable in the air. It was as if time had stood still in that place, where secrets were jealously guarded and the desire to know more was intermingled with the caution of not being discovered. In the midst of this choreography of shadows and flashes, Leah immersed herself in a clandestine world, being attracted by the forbidden magic that this hidden market offered.

In the midst of this mysterious and elusive place, Leah captured the figure of Lucas at the epicenter of that clandestine network. His presence was like a magnet that caught the eyes of everyone around him.

There was something about him, a combination of enigma and charm, that seemed to exert a magnetic power over people. His eyes flashed with the wisdom of one who knows the secrets of a hidden world, and his smile suggested intriguing stories that awaited his gaze, even if he did not dare to utter them.

Lucas stood out in the crowd, an enigmatic figure surrounded by a kind of mystery that attracted everyone's attention. His presence had an uncanny way of commanding respect, but at the same time conveying a sense of closeness. His silences were more eloquent than the words of others; Every gesture of him seemed to contain a whole world of experiences to be explored. It was as if his aura had stories to tell without needing to utter a single word.

Leah moved in the shadows, fascinated by Lucas's mysterious presence in this clandestine environment.

Cautiously, her steps led her toward him, as if a magnet were drawing her toward this walking enigma. She was trying to unravel the mystery that shrouded the enigmatic man. It was evident that behind that piercing gaze and enigmatic smile were intriguing stories. At that moment, Leah felt enveloped by an irrepressible impulse to immerse herself in the secret world that he represented, as if his gesture were a door to an unexplored universe.

Lucas, this mysterious figure seemingly poised on the edge of the ordinary, approached Leah exuding an air of assurance, hinting at something of immense value within her reach. There was an aura about him, an elusive quality that hinted at the safeguarding of a concealed treasure, something profound lying just beneath the surface. When he spoke to her, it was with a gentle tone, as though on the brink of imparting a secret held dear for centuries, his words resonating with echoes of profound and ancient wisdom.

With measured but impactful words, Lucas offered Leah a glimpse into a world that was beyond her imagination, a universe that until that moment was unknown to her. He told her of a place where memories were more than just lived moments; They were like gold coins in an eternal negotiation, where emotions were bought and sold to the highest bidder.

In his words, a parallel universe was interwoven, where past experiences had tangible value and memories, far from being just memories, became coveted assets. It was as if Lucas were showing her a window into a clandestine realm where emotions were transmuted into bargaining chips, a place where nostalgia and longings became commonplace. And in that instant, Leah sensed that a path was opening up before her to a whole new world, a place full of possibilities and dangers, and although cautious, she felt an irresistible curiosity to enter that uncharted territory.

Leah and Lucas, in the middle of a conversation full of suggestions and possibilities shrouded in mystery, immersed the young artist in a tempting idea: the chance to solve her financial problems. Despite the appeal this prospect offered, an unsettling feeling began to grow within her. It was as if an alarm was whispering to her about the risks that awaited her on this new path she was about to embark on. Each step toward that opportunity was mixed with the excitement of change, but also with the fear of the unknown.

The conversation between the two resonated with an air of mystery and timing. Luca's every word was like a tantalizing melody that caressed Leah's ears, offering her a solution to her financial predicament. The idea of finding a way out of her

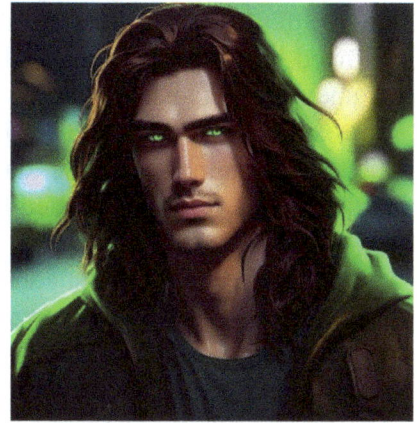

difficulties appealed to her like a magnet, but as she allowed herself to be seduced by that possibility, a sense of uneasiness rose in her chest.

The excitement of a possible solution was intertwined with the perception of a subtle danger lurking beneath the surface. That intuition warned her of the unknown depths to which she was heading. Despite the glimmer of opportunity, she felt the shadow of danger creeping in. It was as if an inner voice was warning her about the risks of stepping into this uncertain terrain, urging her to be cautious before she plunged into the abyss of the unknown. The meeting between Leah and Lucas ended, but for the young artist it was as if a storm of emotions had passed through her being. The revelation of this secret market had acted like a magnet in her spirit, awakening an amalgam of sensations that mixed within her. There was curiosity, that spark that ignited her desire to explore the unknown, to immerse herself in a world that until then had been alien to her.

But also, there was a weight on her shoulders, the weight of a decision that she intuited, could mark a before and after in her life. The enigmatic figure of Lucas and the promise of an underground world filled with exchanges of memories had been etched deep in her mind. It was as if those words and that mysterious atmosphere had sown a seed inside her. A seed that germinated in the form of a choice that could change the course of her existence forever.

Leah was at a crossroads, her heart pounding with the thrill of the unknown and her mind overwhelmed by the possible consequences. It was as if she were standing on the threshold of a new reality, a reality full of uncertainties but also tantalizing promises. That feeling, that crucial moment, became a moment that would remain etched in her memory as the beginning of an uncertain journey, but full of possibilities and profound changes.

Chapter 3

Immersion in
the Underworld

Leah's curiosity was like a powerful magnet that pulled her into the unknown, into that world that was hidden among the bright lights of NeoMind. With a determination burning in her chest to uncover the enigmas of the souvenir market, she returned to the secret place that had become her obsession. She delved deeper into this clandestine sanctuary, ready to explore the dark paths and secrets behind the shadows.

Every step Leah took resonated with a mixture of emotions: excitement and nervousness were intertwined in her being. It felt like she was on a mission, as if she were immersed in a personal quest that pushed her forward, delving deeper into a labyrinth filled with secret transactions and unsolved puzzles. Every move was like deciphering a new riddle in the middle of an unknown world, where every twist revealed hidden layers of this mysterious lattice.

As she moved through the shadows and whispered murmurs, Leah felt adrenaline coursing through her veins. Her heart was pounding, her pulse quickening with anticipation and bewilderment. She was aware that she was entering uncharted territory, a territory where secrets were bought and sold as bargaining chips. But, despite the nervousness that overwhelmed her, a mixture of courage and determination drove her to continue, determined to unravel the mysteries that were hidden in that clandestine underworld.

Every step she took in that clandestine world was like a dance between the fascination and fear that accompanied her every step. She ventured through dark corridors where the glitter of past memories danced in the air, mingled with the sighs of those who offered and bargained for them.

The corridors were imbued with a unique atmosphere, full of secrets and mysteries that slipped through the murmurs of barely audible conversations.

There was an air of caution around every corner, as if the walls themselves were permeated with stories waiting to be discovered. The gestures, the furtive glances and the whispers formed a language of their own, a code that flowed among those who entered that clandestine sanctuary.

For Leah, every detail, every hint of that secret language, was like a piece of a puzzle to be solved. She felt a mixture of intrigue and nervousness, but her curiosity outweighed her fear. She longed to crack that encrypted code, to understand the intricacies of this hidden but tempting world that lay before her. Despite her racing heartbeat, she pressed on, step by step, longing to unveil the secrets behind every whisper and furtive glance in this realm of clandestine exchanges.

Leah was immersed in a sea of other people's emotions that were stirring around her. She watched the transactions in that place, some full of joy while others were steeped in sadness and nostalgia.

Each exchange was like a window into an untold story, a piece of life shared in a barely perceptible whisper that vanished into thin air. It was as if each barter told a different story, revealing a fragment of someone's life, a piece of their history that was lost in the constant flow of place.

Also like witnessing small snippets of other people's existences intertwining in that clandestine place. Some faces exhibited radiant smiles that lit up the air, while others were marked by the weight of nostalgia and sadness. Between these exchanges, Leah perceived how emotions flowed like invisible currents, how each changed object represented something more than a simple memory; It was a little piece of history, a moment frozen in time that had deep meaning for those who shared it.

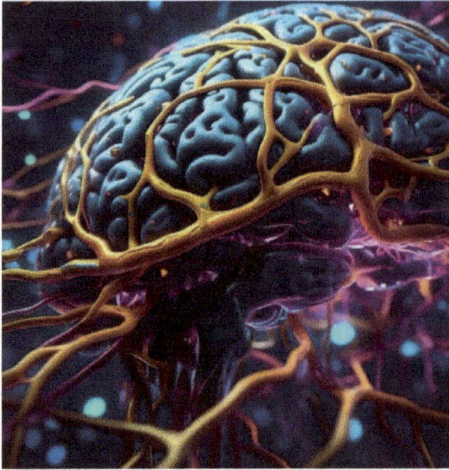

It was as if every deal carried with it a palpable emotional charge, as if she could feel the weight of every memory exchanged in that place.

The multiplicity of sensations enveloped her, immersing her in a world where the feelings of others danced around her, echoing in her own being and awakening in her the curiosity to know more about those lives, those stories intertwined in that clandestine market.

She discovered that behind the apparent simplicity were hidden power structures, subtle hierarchies that governed the flow of transactions. She observed fragile alliances among some businessmen, who smiled diplomatically but hid veiled rivalries under their seemingly cordial exchanges.

In the gloom of that place, her curious eyes caught beyond appearances. She found individuals whose gazes were windows to unknown worlds, holding deep secrets that her lips refused to utter. There was a nonverbal language that she was beginning to decipher: gestures, fleeting glances, subtle movements that spoke for themselves, revealing a web of connections and mysteries that stretched throughout the clandestine compound.

Every encounter, every observation, opened a window into a hidden world, a world where the truth was veiled behind a curtain of silence and enigmatic countenances. She was beginning to glimpse the intricate web of relationships that were woven in that place, understanding that behind every smile could be hidden a network of interests, secrets and subtle pacts that, like invisible threads, connected those who moved in the shadows of that clandestine market.

As Leah immersed herself more in this underworld of exchanges of memories, the risks became clearer to her. She came across fragments of broken pieces of torn lives being offered on the underground market. Some vendors carried the weight of pain with them, marked by the anguish of having let go of a part of their own essence, as if each memory sold was a piece of their being torn away.

On her journey, Leah met buyers whose eyes revealed a remarkable weight, as if they were carrying on their shoulders the burden of acquired other people's memories. Those looks told stories on their own, conveying an emotional charge of experiences that didn't belong to them, but were now part of their being. They were like windows into the soul, showing the weight and intensity of memories that had been exchanged, now carried by those who had acquired them. Each glance spoke of a story, a story that was not told in words, but that was perceived in the deep emotion reflected in those eyes loaded with other people's memory.

Every encounter, every transaction witnessed, was like a blow to Leah, who was beginning to understand the true dimension of that market. She saw beyond the glittering appearances and flashes of tantalizing memories; She entered a territory full of pain, where sellers sacrificed a part of themselves and buyers carried the weight of other people's experiences.

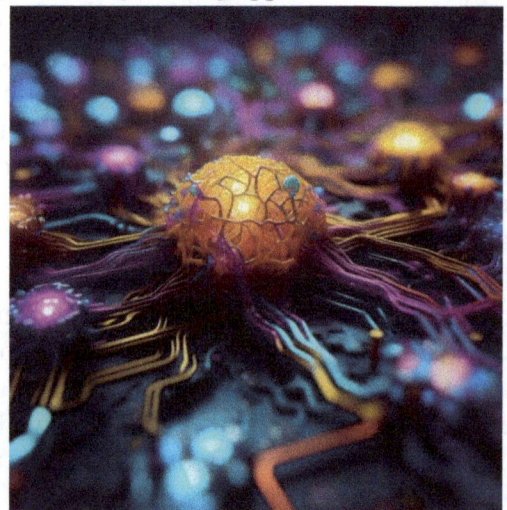

It was a world where emotions were exchanged for coins, but where the price to pay was much higher than it seemed at first glance.

Leah was beginning to realize that she was entering dangerous territory, where ambition and desperate need were intertwined. The ethical and moral complications of that clandestine market unfolded in front of her like a labyrinth with no clear way out, a path where decisions became diffuse and full of dilemmas. The first impression of excitement and discovery vanished in the face of the harsh reality of that hidden world. She was in a place where human passions, such as greed and urgency, dominated reflection and morality. Every exchange, every gesture, showed her the deep complexities that lay beneath the glowing surface of that market.

For Leah, the situation was becoming more and more complicated, she felt the tension between her craving for knowledge and the realization that what she was witnessing did not fit with her principles. She was immersed in an dilemma, where the lines between right and wrong blurred, leaving her trapped in a whirlwind of uncertainty and internal questioning.

Each step she took on that deeper journey brought her closer to understanding the complicated web of that hidden world. However, it also awakened in her a sense of vulnerability, as if she were on a tightrope and the fear of falling invaded her. Despite that uneasy feeling, her determination to uncover the truth that lurked between the intricacies of secret exchanges and the intricacies of the market pushed her to keep moving forward, even if it meant facing the darkest dangers lurking in the shadows.

Every advance, every moment, took her deeper into unknown and dangerous territory. She felt the fragility of her position, as if she were walking on a taut rope over an abyss of uncertainty.

Despite the fear growing inside her, she was determined to keep going. She felt that each discovery, no matter how dangerous, brought her a little closer to the truth hidden behind this underworld.

Chapter 4

The Shadow of the Merchant of Instants

The enigmatic Merchant of Instants was like a locked door in the secret world of NeoMind, a puzzle that Leah couldn't resist trying to solve. It was as if the city's very heart hid behind this mysterious figure, and she felt an urgent need to uncover the secrets this enigma held. Day in and day out, her thoughts revolved around this quest, driven by an intense desire to demystify the character that seemed to hold the answers to NeoMind's deepest mysteries. The search for the Merchant's identity had grown into an all-consuming passion, fueled by Leah's unrelenting curiosity and her relentless pursuit of the truth

The Merchant of Instants was like a moving shadow, always elusive and difficult to follow. Every attempt to discover his true identity was like catching a glimmer in the dark: frustrating and elusive. His presence was felt in the whispers of the most secretive business, in the most mysterious transactions, but his face and his name seemed to be shrouded in an impenetrable veil.

For Leah, this search was a challenge that awakened her most inquisitive instinct. Every piece of information about this enigmatic character was like a piece of the puzzle that refused to fit together. As she tracked him down, the obsession to learn his identity morphed into a personal mission, a mission that propelled her to unravel the deepest secrets and confront the intricate web of mysteries surrounding the Merchant of Instants in the clandestine world of NeoMind.

She, in the midst of the hustle of the city, caught a barely whispered clue that led her to follow in the footsteps of the elusive Merchant. She moved among the old sellers and frequent buyers, searching for any clue that might decipher the Merchant's riddle, a mystery shrouded in shadows.

It was like a game of clues, where every move of those around her could be a key piece in solving the riddle. Every word, was like a piece of a puzzle that Leah was trying to put together to unravel the mystery of the Merchant.

She probed with curious glances and careful questions, looking for patterns between the interactions and movements of those who might have some knowledge of the Merchant. She observed the subtle changes in expressions, the sudden pauses in conversations, and the furtive glances that crossed between the underground traders. Every inflection in her voice, became a clue that she was trying to fit into the puzzle of this enigma.

Despite her determination, the information seemed to vanish through her fingers like fine sand. The rumors were like wisps of grass slipping through the alleys of the city, leaving it with more questions than answers.

However, she didn't give up. Every single word she heard, every little gesture she observed, brought her a step closer to unraveling the identity of the mysterious Merchant of Instants. It was like collecting puzzle pieces – each small detail mattered, edging her nearer to the truth she was so determined to find.

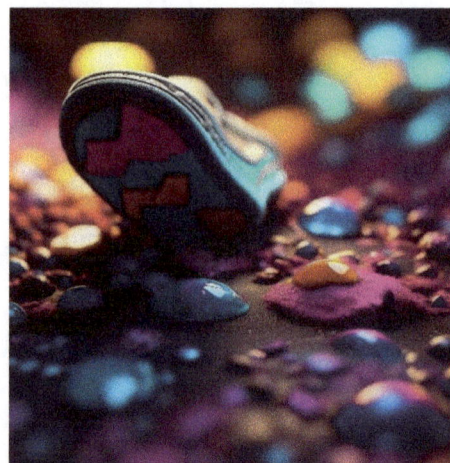

Every conversation, represented an additional step toward the truth, even if it subtly faded away, like water dripping through one's fingers. The Merchant of Instants remained

enigmatic, as if intertwined in the most elusive corners of NeoMind, visible but always out of reach. Every attempt to decipher his identity was like chasing shadows that slithered through the alleys of the city, escaping just when they seemed to be within arm's reach.

Every attempt to obtain information about the Merchant was like catching a breeze in one's hands: fleeting and elusive.

The clues she expected to find seemed to vanish into thin air, leaving her feeling like she was chasing shadows. The Merchant's identity was like a well-kept secret that refused to be revealed, as if he were wrapped up in a web of untouchable mysteries.

Despite her tireless efforts to unravel this enigma, each attempt seemed to bring her closer and farther away at the same time. The truth about the Merchant of Instants was present, but the veil that hid it held firm, preventing him from capturing it completely. It was as if this enigmatic character was intertwined with the very essence of NeoMind, visible to the naked eye but challenging to reach.

Leah immersed herself in a complex labyrinth of enigmas, chasing clues that were unraveling before her eyes. She ventured into the most enigmatic places in the city, where shadows came to life and whispers of secrets floated in the air like bargaining chips.

Each hint followed was like following the trail of a firefly in the dark; barely visible before disappearing, leaving Leah in search of the next lost clue.

She followed every hint, that suggested a possible clue to the elusive Merchant of Instants. Her steps led her to the most remote places, where rumor became reality and reality disguised itself as shadows. She wandered into narrow alleys and forgotten squares, where glances seemed to whisper secrets and gestures contained stories that were hidden under the light of NeoMind.

Every time Leah set out on a quest, it was like opening a box full of new puzzles. Every corner explored was a chance to uncover a crucial clue that would lead to the Merchant. Although the tracks seemed to slip away like bubbles in the wind, she wouldn't give up. She moved steadily forward, into the darkest corners of the city, eager to unveil the truth behind this increasingly intricate enigma.

With each clue discovered, the image of the Merchant was drawn more clearly in Leah's mind, though it remained a puzzle without enough pieces to complete it. There was something about the elusive figure that stirred a mixture of intrigue and fear in her, a presence that seemed to have influence in the most crucial dealings of the underground market.

Each clue kept adding small details to the Merchant's portrait: subtle gestures, fleeting mentions, ambiguous stories. They were loose pieces that, although they didn't quite fit, helped to form a blurred outline of who this enigmatic character was. But, despite getting closer to deciphering his identity, the sense persisted that something fundamental was still slipping away, a crucial piece that was still hidden in the shadows.

The figure of the Merchant became an intriguing and at the same time disturbing enigma for Leah.

She felt his presence seem to weave into the most elusive threads of the underground market, as if his influence extended beyond simple transactions, unleashing an aura of mystery and power that blended with the shadows of NeoMind. It was a disconcerting sensation, for the nearer she came to meeting the Merchant, the more the depth of his mystery was revealed, awakening in her a fascination and, at the same time, an incessant uneasiness.

The stories being told in the city, the gossip that flowed in the alleys, and the connections between those who kept secrets seemed to converge toward an unsettling truth. The shadow of the Merchant of Instants loomed like an ominous presence that manipulated the hidden threads of the underground market, weaving a web of influence that stretched beyond the obvious.

The urban legends surrounding the Merchant were like threads that were woven into a tapestry of mysteries.

The rumors whispered in the most remote places, the glances that crossed with complicity, the words that barely touched the surface of what was said, everything pointed to a reality darker and more complex than it seemed.

Leah listened intently to the clandestine conversations, trying to piece together the scattered bits of information that formed a more complete picture of the Merchant. There was an unsettling sensation in the air, as if the shadow of this enigmatic individual stretched beyond what was visible to the naked eye. He seemed to control a power that went beyond the usual transactions, weaving a web of influence that stretched into every dark corner of NeoMind. It was a truth that was intuited rather than seen, a presence that evoked both fear and curiosity in those who sought to decipher its mystery.

Each advance in the Merchant's quest brought Leah a little closer to the truth she longed for, but at the same time plunged her into a sea of mysteries and risks.

Every sign, pointed to an imminent revelation, an imminent confrontation with a figure whose true essence could alter the course of her investigation and her life forever.

With each step forward, the feeling of being closer to the Merchant mingled with the palpable tension in the air. The signs she followed seemed to converge toward a critical point, a crossroads where the truth was about to emerge from the shadows. It was as if she were on the very edge of discovering something momentous, something that would transform her understanding of the world around her.

However, along with the anticipation of the revelation, there was also a latent uneasiness.The idea of coming face-to-face with the Merchant brought with it a mixture of emotions: expectation, but also understandable fear.

She was aware that what she discovered in that encounter could radically change her perspective and mark a before and after in her life.

She felt the weight of the unknown on her shoulders, knowing that every step she took took her away from the comfort of the familiar and plunged her deeper into uncharted territory, full of intrigue and risk.

Chapter 5

Alliances and Mistrust

Amid the tangle of secrets and hidden transactions, Leah felt the need to find allies she could trust as she pursued the truth behind the underground souvenir market. It was at that moment that her path crossed with that of Anais, an enigmatic figure, marked by exile from the system and shrouded in mystery, which sowed doubts about her true intentions.

Anais presented herself as an enigma on Leah's path. Anais's deep gaze hid more than it revealed, and her words were measured, as if they carried with them the weight of hidden truths. There was a sense of caution that crept into the air whenever Anais was around, as if her presence was marked by an enigmatic past.

Leah was attracted by Anais enigmatic presence, captivated by the possibility of finding in her a reliable ally in her search.

However, the shadows that surrounded Anais, her calculated gestures and her history marked by exile from the system, also sowed doubts in Leah´s mind. Was Anais a true ally in her search for the truth or did she hide motives behind her enigmatic façade The uncertainty added to the mystery surrounding the figure of this new companion on her way to the revelation of the clandestine market of memories.

Anais exuded a cautious demeanor, her wisdom a product of weathering through tough times. There was a unique allure in her manner, drawing the focus of those delving into the shadows of NeoMind, seeking answers and guidance. Her aura held a compelling charm, inviting the weary and curious alike, hinting at a depth of insight born from traversing the city's enigmatic passages.

Anais's presence was like a magnet for those who longed to understand the secrets of the city.

There was something about her, perhaps in her eyes that held untold stories, or in her posture, full of a profound serenity, that attracted the curiosity of those who ventured into the most elusive places of the metropolis. Also shrouded in a kind of experience that seemed to have been carved by adversity. Anais was like a beacon in the darkness, a source of knowledge for those who dared to seek answers in the most unexpected places. Her presence not only aroused interest, but also a sense that behind her words and gestures was hidden a vast knowledge accumulated through difficult experiences.

Leah and Anais found a surprising bond, a union born out of a shared urgency to unravel the truth behind the secret deals. Still, in this world of intertwined memories and deception around every corner, everyone's intentions, including Anais, became unknown.

The connection between Lia and Anais grew rapidly, fueled by a shared determination to unravel the mysteries surrounding the underground market. However, as they progressed together, doubts about Anais's true motivations crept into Leah's mind. Was Anais truly committed to the search for truth or was there something more behind her desire to uncover the secrets of NeoMind? In a world where trust was as fragile as a sigh, Leah was faced with the challenge of deciphering whether she could fully trust her new ally.

Anais, the exile of the system, became a kind of guide for Leah, revealing dark aspects of the market and pointing out paths that could lead her to the very center of the clandestine network. However, Anais's words and actions left a trail of doubts and suspicions on Leah's path.

Whenever Anais shared her knowledge, there was a tinge of mystery in her words, as if she was keeping key information behind a curtain of enigmas.

Despite being a guide in this labyrinth of secrets, her actions left a veil of uncertainty about her true intentions. Was she sharing the whole truth, or were there aspects that she deliberately hid? The shadow of distrust crept subtly into Leah's mind, causing her to question the depth of the alliance they had formed. Though the caution signs flickered, Leah's urgency to discover the truth dazzled her prudence. She plunged further into the web of mysteries and dangers, trusting the data provided by Anais, but keeping a constant watch on her companion's true intentions.

With every step forward, Leah felt the weight of uncertainty. Despite trusting Anais's indications in part, her intuition reminded her to keep a watchful eye, as if she were walking a tightrope between trust and distrust. Desperation to unravel NeoMind's secrets drove her, but every revelation and hint left a shadow of suspicion over her ally's true motivations.

It was a delicate dance between moving forward with determination and maintaining caution, a fine line that Leah struggled to balance in her search for truth.

Every time Leah met Anais, it was like dancing on a tightrope between trust and distrust. The revelations she shared plunged her into the depths of the intricate hidden marketplace, unmasking some secrets, but also stoked uncertainty about whether she could fully trust her loyalty and ultimate goals.

Anais's words were like flashes of light illuminating dark corners of the underground market, revealing crucial information for Leah's journey to the truth. Behind each revelation, however, lurked a glimmer of ambiguity, a feeling that perhaps she wasn't revealing everything she knew. Doubts about her motives and the depth of her commitment to Leah's cause persisted, creating an enigma that the young artist struggled to decipher.

It was a constant dance between taking advantage of the valuable information provided by Anais and keeping her guard up, aware that each revelation could hide more than it showed.

In every corner of NeoMind, gazes hid insatiable desires and whispers concealed impenetrable intentions. Alliances were woven with fragile threads, interests fluctuated like the wind and truth became a currency as valuable as the memories that were traded. On the bustling streets of NeoMind, each individual had their own game going on, each with their own strategy and hidden goals. Behind the diplomatic smiles and friendly gestures, there were indecipherable ambitions, lust for power, and desires for control. The city vibrated with an unsettling energy, a constant dance between those who coveted information and those willing to offer it in exchange for favors or benefits of their own.

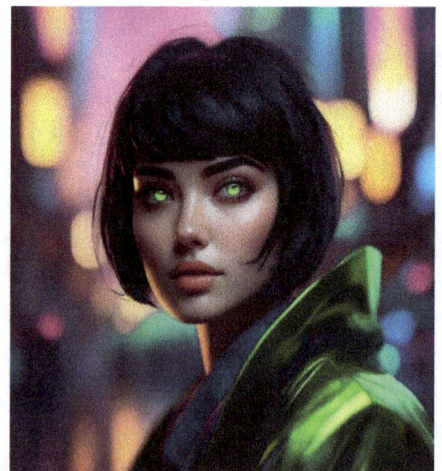

The paths to truth were shrouded in shadows and mistrust, every step had to be measured, and every alliance carefully weighed in an urban landscape where cunning and ambition reigned unfettered.

Leah was immersed in a risky game, balancing herself between the illusion of discovering the truth and the lingering shadow of mistrust. Each advance with Anais brought her closer to the long-awaited revelation, but it also plunged her into an abyss of doubts about who her true allies and enemies were in that world full of intrigue and ambiguity.

Every encounter with Anais was a journey full of expectations and fears. Leah clung to each revelation like a glimmer of light in the darkness, though the shadow of uncertainty always lurked in her mind, questioning whether Anais was a reliable guide or just another cog in a complicated game of self-interest.

In that universe of intrigues, every step forward was a risky bet, with no certainty about who was friend or foe in that labyrinth of intersecting interests.

Chapter 6

Customers and
Their Stories

In every corner of the hidden market of memories, stories woven with threads of life, love, pain, and hope were hidden. For Leah, each transaction was not just an economic exchange, but a window into the fragments of the soul that were revealed with each memory sold.

Every barter in that clandestine place was much more than just a business. It was like briefly observing someone's heart, as if the pieces of their past lives were unraveling in each shared memory. In that market, memories weren't just digital data or empty images; They were pieces of experiences, pieces of identity given in exchange for a coin. For Leah, each sale and purchase was a constant reminder of the depth and complexity of the human being, embodied in the memories they exchanged as if they were precious treasures.

With each step deeper into this world, she stumbled upon a gallery of clients, each with stories that painted the complexity of the human being in its most sincere and real state.

Each individual carried the weight of their choices, the pain of their farewells or the ephemeral bliss of unforgettable moments.

For Leah, each face in that clandestine market told a unique story. There were those who carried in their eyes the melancholy of what they had lost, others, the spark of what they had loved and enjoyed. The customers were more than buyers: they were itinerant storytellers, carrying with them a lifetime in fragments of memories. Between those hallways, every interaction was a fleeting glimpse into the lives of others, a reminder that behind every memory there was a story to tell, whether it was love, regret, or the struggle to find meaning in the chaos of existence.

There was an old man, he recalled a moment of youth and lost love, his face lit up as if time were going backwards. And then there was that woman, whose eyes reflected the longing for a hug, she could no longer experience, sold to ease the unbearable weight of financial debt.

The older man carried with him the echo of a past that still beat in his heart. Every time he spoke of those moments of youth and romance, his countenance transformed, as if he were reliving those days full of vitality and love. A spark shone in his eyes that only the most cherished memories can ignite.

The woman, on the other hand, conveyed a silent sadness. Her eyes spoke of a deep pain, a longing for contact that was no longer within reach.

Every time she spoke about the embrace she had lost and that now existed only in the form of a memory, her gaze was plunged into a painful nostalgia, as if she were reliving the absence of that affectionate gesture that she longed to feel again.

Each story, whether moving or full of hope, showed the delicacy and resilience that dwells in the human heart. Despite their differences, all the customers shared an invisible bond: they were looking for relief, a way to escape, or even find redemption through the sale of their most cherished memories.

The stories that flowed into that market were like a tapestry of life itself, each with its own unique hues and textures. Some sought to free themselves from a weight, as if the act of getting rid of their memories would allow them to breathe lighter. Others longed to escape, to find a way out of the emotional or financial labyrinths that seemed to drown them.

And among those stories, there were also those who sought redemption, as if the act of selling their memories was an attempt to start over, leaving behind a chapter they wished to forget or transform.

Each of them, in their diversity, shared that basic human need: to seek a respite, a relief or even a way to remake themselves through the exchange of the most intimate, those pieces of life enclosed in their most precious memories. It was as if every memoir offered for sale was an attempt to reconstruct itself or at least find solace in the midst of its personal struggles.

Leah was like an observer of other people's lives, witnessing the profound relationship between human experiences and the memories that accompanied them. Each negotiation was like an unfolded window into the complexity of the human being, a lesson in the fleeting nature of happiness and the perennial burden of loss.

Every exchange she witnessed was like a painting portraying the different faces of existence. She watched as people shared their memories, some filled with joy and others tinged with sadness, showing that happiness is often fleeting and moments of sadness can linger like tattoos on the soul.

In these dealings, Leah discovered the fragility of joy, ephemeral as the glimmer of a shooting star, and the painful permanence of loss, engraved in the human heart.

It was as if each agreement was a master class in the human condition, a deep look at the complexity of emotions and experiences. Leah learned about the ephemeral nature of bliss, which often fades away like a melody that ends too soon, and the eternal burden carry for loss, like shadows.

The painful stories echoed in her heart, leaving a mark that could not be erased.

Sadness and faith were linked in a continuous back-and-forth, reminding her that behind every memory sold was hidden a unique and profound journey of the human being.

Each story struck the most sensitive chords of Leah. Suffering, raw and real, was mixed with hope, as if they were two opposite poles joined by an invisible thread.

Every time she heard those stories, it was as if she was witnessing the very essence of humanity, with its struggles, its falls, and its attempts to get up again and again. It was as if memories were portals to the souls of those who sold them. In each memory, she saw the struggle, resilience, and persistence of those who had traversed paths full of obstacles. Tears and smiles, woven together into a tapestry

of human emotions, reminded Leah that each memory sold carried with it a universe of unique experiences, a unique story of love, loss, resilience, and hope.

Leah faced dilemmas in every story she witnessed, questioning the true value of memories and the ethics of those who bought or sold them.

Each customer who entered that market carried with them a unique story, an amalgam of intertwined emotions that made each deal more than just a transaction. For Leah, it was like stepping into a labyrinth of dilemmas, where every memory offered raised questions about the true cost of memory.

She was immersed in a sea of questions: what was the true value of a past experience? Could the essence of a memory be quantified? The motivations of those who bought or sold souvenirs, sometimes driven by nostalgia, sometimes by the search for a solution to financial problems, plunged Leah into a whirlwind of reflections on the ethics behind that clandestine market.

Each story made her question whether this exchange of memories was an act of liberation or a kind of sale of the soul.

Each story, with its nuances and whispers of other people's lives, was like an echo that resonated in the depths of her being. Leah was at a crossroads, where each story raised questions about her own actions and her role in the ever-changing scenario. The complexity of these exchanges not only challenged her perception of the value of memories, but also forced her to question the moral implications of her participation in a world where the past was sold as a commodity.

Each account reminded her that her presence in that market was not just a search for answers or a fight for her own survival, but a foray into the very essence of humanity. The stories she heard were not just fragments of memory, they were testimonies of lives, dreams, loves and pains, each leaving an indelible mark on her consciousness, challenging her to reflect on the ultimate meaning of her choices and her participation in that turbulent world.

Chapter 7

The Information Leak

Inside the underground market, an unsettling rumor was spreading like wildfire: a leak was jeopardizing the secure foundations that had kept the transactions of the most precious memorabilia secret.

It was as if a dark shadow had crept into the aisles of the market, sowing fear among merchants and shoppers. The haunting murmurs echoed, warning of a possible breach in the veil of secrecy that had protected the secret transactions. The once quiet and clandestine atmosphere was now shaken by anxiety and uncertainty.

The usual hum of the market had been transformed into a heavy, anxiety-laden silence. Leah could feel the atmosphere becoming rarefied, as if the whole place was on the verge of collapse. News of the leak spread like wildfire, generating an uproar among merchants and buyers. The security that had once been a protective wall for the most private stories now hung in the balance.

The shadows cast on the walls seemed more unsettling, as if the darkness itself was whispering secrets that had previously remained hidden. Nervousness flowed in every gesture, in every furtive glance that was exchanged between those who had made the market their world. The threat of the revelation of private stories loomed like a storm, capable of wiping out the trust built on years of hidden transactions.

Leah was enveloped in a rarefied environment, a scenario where uncertainty reigned supreme. Unanswered questions hung in the thick air, as the future of the underground market hung in the balance, vulnerable to a potential breakup that could change the lives of everyone involved forever.

The atmosphere became dense, as if an invisible electric current had altered the atmosphere of those alleys. Leah noticed how even the air itself seemed to contain a sigh of anxiety.

Merchants and buyers, once so confident, now moved cautiously, as if every move could reveal a secret or trigger a catastrophe.

The echoed footsteps, amplifying the tension that floated in the shadows. The conversations, once full of trust, were now held on a fragile thread of caution. Every word whispered was a risk, every transaction, a gamble with fate. Uncertainty had crept into every corner, weaving a veil of worry that obscured even the most intimate moments of the underground market.

The echo of rumors spread rapidly, pointing to a possible breach in the strength of the underground market. The certainty that once protected every exchange was crumbling, generating widespread unease among those who had relied on the veil of secrecy and confidentiality.

The word "escape" echoed through the murmurs, sowing distrust among merchants and regular buyers. A sense of uneasiness gripped the air, as if every shadow hid an unknown danger.

Paranoia crept into the minds of those who once felt safe in that market, questioning every step and every interaction in a scenario now obscured by doubt and suspicion.

The atmosphere became more fraught with tension, every gesture was scrutinized and every glance was filled with suspicion. The sellers looked suspiciously at the buyers, as if their intentions were shrouded in a blanket of doubt. Buyers, in turn, were wary of middlemen, questioning every word and move as if they were hiding some secret.

In that landscape of uncertainty, each person became an enigma to be solved. Each individual was under the magnifying glass of mistrust in a scenario where the rules

of the game became blurred and previous alliances dissolved like figures of smoke. It was a chessboard on which the pieces moved without a clear pattern, plunging everyone into a constant state of alert.

The atmosphere was charged with palpable tension, as if they were on the brink of a storm ready to break loose. The fear was not only focused on the risk of being discovered by the authorities lurking in the shadows, but also on the fragility of those whose memories became bargaining chips in that dark market.

Every exchange, every memory sold, seemed to carry with it an overwhelming emotional charge. The fear lay not only in the threat of being caught in the web of secrets, but also in the vulnerability of those who confided their most intimate experiences to strangers, turning their memories into a currency whose value went beyond the monetary.

The pressure was mounting around her, not only did the leak undermine the anonymity of the underground market, but it put every individual who was part of it at risk.

The responsibility weighed heavily on they conscience. The threat of the leak not only affected those seeking an escape through memories, but became a latent danger that loomed over every corner of that clandestine world.

Each moment added a piece to the puzzle of information leakage. Every step Leah took amid the murmurs and nervous glances brought her closer to the heart of the mystery. She searched for signs between the half-finished conversations, trying to decipher the whispers that hung in the air, trying to piece together the sequence of events that had triggered the breakdown in the security of the underground market.

Every second became an urgent echo in the clock that marked the time, each exchange was a rapid heartbeat in Leah's chest. In every gesture, she glimpsed the approaching danger, a danger that threatened to tear apart the fragile security that had guarded the deepest secrets.

Discovering the source of the leak became a desperate race against the constant ticking of the clock, a feverish quest to safeguard the confidentiality of stories that slipped through greedy hands in that obscure market of memories.

Chapter 8

The Nature
of Memories

Leah plunged even deeper into her investigation, determined to uncover the truth behind the true nature of the memories and the emotional impact that underlay each clandestine exchange.

Leah immersed herself in a relentless search that led her to uncover hidden details, to question deep-rooted beliefs and to question the true essence of what memories meant in that clandestine market. Her days became one of constant inquiry, unearthing secrets under every stone and challenging accepted notions about the value of those memories.

Leah soon realized that the memories weren't just images stored on devices, they were living bits of the human soul. They represented emotions, connections and experiences encapsulated in a tangible form, capable of causing a deep emotional impact on both those who sold them and those who acquired them. They were much more than just snapshots; They were the very essence of life and human connections, wrapped up in every memory.

Leah came across stories of sellers burdened by the loss of part of their essence, of buyers desperately seeking to fill emotional voids, but also of those whose lives had been transformed by the acquisition of other people's memories.

The very nature of memories was far more complex than She had imagined. They weren't just digital files; They were mirrors of the human soul, bearers of emotions, traumas, and joys. Each carried with it an emotional weight that resonated beyond memory itself, influencing the lives and identities of those who possessed them.

The discovery of this hidden truth opened a door to a deeper understanding of the connection between memories and the very essence of humanity. For Leah, this revelation was transformative. Understanding the true nature of memories led her to rethink her own beliefs. Her motivations, and the impact of her tireless search for truth in the midst of that underground market.

She found herself questioning the real price of the information she sought and the emotional impact it had on the individuals involved in the intricate web of memory exchanges.

Chapter 9

Facing the Merchant

Determined to uncover the truth about the Merchant of Instants, Leah embarked on a mission that led her to explore every dark corner of NeoMind. Every step she took seemed to bring her closer to the heart of the enigma, but at the same time, the uncertainty about who this mysterious character really was grew greater, as if each new clue added more layers of mystery instead of revealing the Merchant's true identity and motives.

Following barely visible signs and fuzzy clues, Leah entered a game full of surprises that challenged her in the search for the Merchant. Rumors and whispers insinuated that this enigmatic individual had deep connections to the most significant events of the underground market, but his real reasons remained hidden behind a veil of mystery.

Each teaser seemed to throw up more questions than answers, plunging Leah into a labyrinth of unknowns that intertwined in an intriguing game of secrets.

Every step toward the encounter with the Merchant of Instants seemed to plunge her into a labyrinth of complications. Along the way, she encountered insurmountable obstacles, such as guards and representatives who zealously guarded the enigmatic figure who ran the underground market. Despite her steadfast determination, she found herself facing insurmountable walls and unwavering loyalty from those who protected the enigmatic leader. Each attempt was transformed into a struggle between her unbreakable will and the well-organized defenses that guarded the elusive Merchant.

The Merchant always seemed to anticipate, leaving behind him a thick veil of mystery. Every time Leah approached, she encountered unexpected surprises and ingenious schemes that redirected her efforts to paths that led nowhere. Each advance was followed by an unexpected twist, as if the Merchant had mapped out an intricate labyrinth to deflect his attempts.

Despite the challenges, her desire for answers did not wane; Each barrier strengthened her resolve.

Not only did she yearn for answers for herself, she also sought justice for those who had been affected by the dark entanglements of that market. She wanted to confront the Merchant not just out of curiosity, but to give a voice to those who had been silenced by the shadows of that underground world.

Facing the challenges in her path, Leah had to rethink every step in her quest. The confrontation with the Merchant became more difficult, but also more pressing as the enigma closed around her. Each failed tactic pushed her to reconsider her approach, knowing that time was running out and the web of secrets was tightening, making every move crucial.

Every challenge, no matter how surprising, only fueled Leah's determination. Her search became a risky game of ingenuity and perseverance, where each attempt to reach the enigmatic leader of the underground market seemed to bring her closer to a truth that would transform her vision of the world.

Each step in her journey increased the intensity of her efforts, knowing that what she discovered could alter her understanding of the reality she knew.

Chapter 10

The Pieces of
the Puzzle

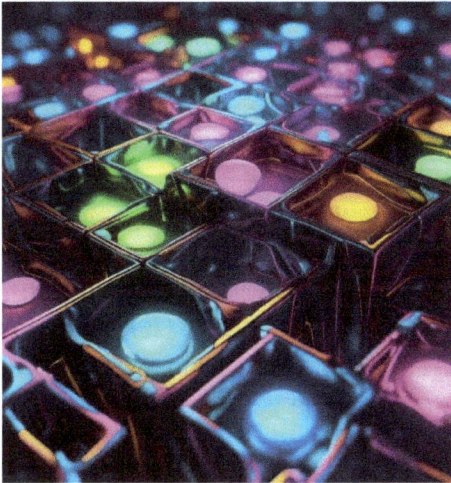

Leah immersed herself in the search, piecing together the pieces of a complex enigma. Each answer found was like a beacon illuminating a new mystery, leading it deeper into a labyrinth of unsolved questions. With determination, she set about connecting each piece, but for every one that fit, two others seemed to emerge, multiplying the challenge of reaching complete understanding. Each breakthrough was a new puzzle waiting to be solved.

Every trail followed, every talk held, and every clue found were like pieces of a giant puzzle, the enigma of the Merchant of Instants and his secret market. But as Leah gathered those cards, each answer she got uncovered more questions, hidden in dark corners that tested even her firmest persistence. Each advance seemed to open a new path full of mysteries.As she went along piecing the clues together, she stumbled upon puzzling revelations that further complicated the scenario she was exploring. The relationships she found between the important characters of the secret market showed a web of connections, agreements, and betrayals that went far beyond what she expected. Each discovery seemed to take her deeper into a labyrinth of complicated relationships and intertwined secrets.

As she found new clues, she was faced with ethical dilemmas that made her question the motivations of the people around her. Every truth she uncovered shook her foundations, challenging what she thought she knew about the occult market and how it affected those connected to it. She was trying to understand the implications of her discoveries on the lives of those involved in this intricate world. Each solution to one mystery posed three more, as if each revelation were the beginning of a tangled dance of secrets.

Each step forward seemed to be tinged with more questions, as the shadows of mystery lengthened in their path.Leah was in a constant back-and-forth between feeling that she was closer to understanding the truth and, at the same time, noticing how that total understanding seemed to recede. Each step forward seemed to bring more questions than answers, as if the knowledge she gained plunged her into a whirlwind of certainties and doubts. The paradox of feeling close but far from the truth impelled her to keep searching, longing for clearer and more decisive answers that seemed to

elude her at every turn.Every time a piece of the puzzle fell into place, Leah felt herself plunged into even more intricate territory, as if she were navigating a dark labyrinth where the truth was elusive. Each answer was a flash that illuminated an area, but at the same time, generated a swarm of new questions that pushed her forward.

Her tireless quest to unravel the mystery surrounding the Merchant of Instants and the underground market of memories was like chasing a reflection in a shifting mirage.

Chapter 11

The Emotional Cost

The memories, which once seemed like mere pieces in a hidden market, now took on a new shape before Leah's eyes. As she dug for answers, she discovered the crushing emotional weight that each memory brought with it. She saw how those who sold and bought these fragments of life carried with them an indescribable burden. Sellers, stripped of their own experiences, were scarred by loss, and buyers, seeking a kind of salvation in the memories of others, also carried with them an emotional burden that was not theirs. The truth stood before Leah, not just as a mere revelation, but as a heart-wrenching reflection of human pain and the complexity of existence itself.

The vendors, once shadowy figures in the market, now revealed themselves in a different way before Leah's eyes. A trace of emptiness could be glimpsed in their faces, once anonymous, as if something essential had vanished.

Every time they sold a souvenir, something inside them seemed to fade away, as if part of their essence was shed with each transaction. Although it was not visible to the naked eye, there was a deep imprint on their souls, an invisible but deep mark, like scars that are not seen but felt deep within their being.

Watching, Leah, felt the weight of anguish in each of those who released their dearest memories. Their accounts were like stories marked by scars, showing the pain and loneliness that accompanied each deal. The tears, barely visible but deep, and the suppressed sighs told of the emotional charge that remained with them, even after they had exchanged their memories. It was as if part of their being vanished, leaving a void that words could not fill.

Buyers, with their eagerness to fill emotional gaps or escape previous torments, faced the side effects of acquired memories.

Some were immersed in a tangle of other people's emotions, unable to handle the added weight of their own experiences. Others, wracked by guilt or remorse, were caught up in a whirlwind of memories that didn't belong to them, consuming their own identity in the process. It was as if they were carrying an alien weight that pressed on their souls and made them hostage to experiences they could not control.

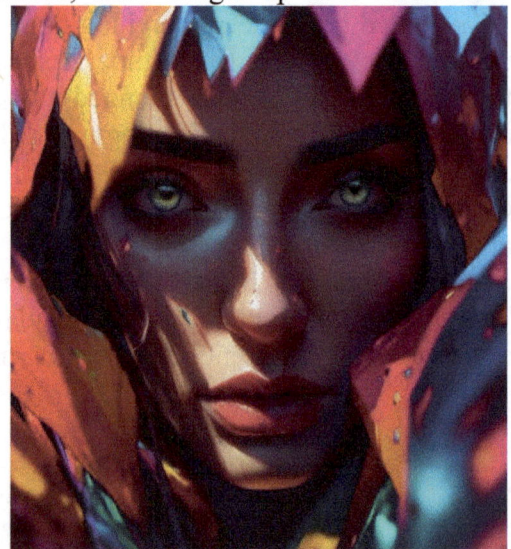

In this clandestine market, it was not only memoirs that were traded; It was a barter that involved the very being of the people. The transaction of memories had an emotional cost that exceeded any previous expectations. It was as if every memory sold or bought left a deep imprint on the soul, a mark that transcended the simple exchange of experiences.

It was like surrendering a part of oneself, a piece of identity that was detached and suspended in an emotional limbo. The weight of these transactions went beyond material value; It was a barter of emotions, of connections with the past and with the most intimate part of each individual.

Leah was in a whirlwind of inner dilemmas as she witnessed these silent torments. Her relentless search for truth was intertwined with a growing moral urgency. Seeing the tragedies, feeling the weight of the stories in the eyes of those affected, pushed her into an inner conflict. Should she continue to unravel the mystery in pursuit of the truth, or should she stop this chain of suffering that the exchanges of memories were leaving in their wake? She felt the need to speak out, to be the spokesperson for those whose lives were shattered by the emotional impact of these clandestine dealings.

Every harrowing account she witnessed sowed a seed of responsibility in his heart, an urgent call to action to stop the cycle of despair that marked the lives of so many.

Leah's perception was broadened as she discovered the profound impact not only on the sellers, but also on the buyers of the underground market.

Chapter 12

The Net Narrows

The underground market, once hidden in the darkest folds, now felt the weight of the pressure that was hanging over it. The fence was tightening, as if the shadow that had protected it was slowly dissipating. Authorities and other outside forces were reaching out with determination, willing to penetrate the deeper layers of the exchanges of memories that had permeated NeoMind. It was as if the opacity that had been it´s shield was gradually disappearing, exposing every previously hidden corner. The market, once shrouded in secrecy, now faced imminent exposure in the light of public scrutiny.

Leah was immersed in a growing web of risks and threats, accompanied by the allies she had encountered along the way. Every step they took, every word whispered, seemed to be scrutinized, as if under the constant gaze of invisible eyes. This scrutiny not only threatened their investigation, but also compromised their own safety.

The feeling of being constantly watched added a layer of palpable tension to every interaction, turning every gesture into a potential risk to them and their mission.

Leah and her companion, firm in their purpose of dismantling the network of the clandestine market, were immersed in a frantic race against the clock. In the midst of this maelstrom, alliances were strengthened, woven by the urgency of the situation. Each finding, each clue followed, brought them closer to the very bowels of the clandestine network, but at the same time, exposed them to ever greater risks. Every step toward the truth was a stepping stone into increasingly dangerous terrain, where uncertainty and threat lurked around every corner.

The enigmatic figure of the Merchant of Instants stood as the epicenter of this intricate network, unfolding a labyrinthine network of protections and countermeasures. Every effort to approach it became a complex labyrinth, deceptive paths, and carefully orchestrated traps.

Every attempt at rapprochement seemed to be an illusion, a ruse that challenged the skill and steadfastness of Leah and her allie. It was like facing an enigma with infinite layers, where every step led to a dead end, constantly challenging her ingenuity and determination.

With each planned strategy, the dangers multiplied. The atmosphere was charged with tension, as if every step taken translated into an exponential increase in risk. Uncertainty became the only certainty in this volatile scenario, where every strategic move resounded like a discordant note in an already tense environment full of latent dangers.

They found themselves at a crossroads, on the edge between unraveling the sinister market and the unsettling certainty that each advance brought them closer to the abyss. Each move seemed to come full circle, but it also cornered them, pushing them toward crucial decisions.

In the heat of persecution and constant pressure, the resolve of Leah and her companion remained unwavering. Despite the imminent risks, their goal of dismantling this clandestine network remained firm, fueled by the conviction to reveal the truth.

Chapter 13

Difficult Decisions

At the center of this whirlwind of pressure and danger surrounding her relentless search for the truth, Leah faced a constant dilemma. Every step she took and every choice she made represented an ethical crossroads that tested her integrity. The decisions she made were like paths that opened up before her, each carrying with it the burden of its consequences. Each choice was a scale on which her principles were weighed, while the weight of her determinations fell on her shoulders, constantly reminding her of the responsibility that came with each step on this intricate path to truth.

The ethical dilemma became a constant shadow on her way to dismantling the underground market. She found herself at crossroads where the temptation to justify methods by results was overwhelming, but the moral price became clearer with each decision.

How far did she have to go to achieve her goal without tarnishing her integrity? Each choice was a delicate balance between the conviction to do the right thing and the pressure to pursue the truth, and each step reminded her of the importance of standing firm in her principles, even in the most challenging of times.

Tough decisions piled up as the risk grew. The difference between what seemed right and what didn't became blurred in a field of dilemmas. Each choice not only weighed on her own conscience, but also resonated in the lives of those around her. Each step was a labyrinth of doubts and consequences, where the weight of doing the right thing often clashed with the urgency of reaching for the truth.

The pressure to get answers clashed with the weight of their values. Should she risk the safety of a few to protect the many?

In this tense environment and with the clock ticking against her, Leah was caught up in the difficult task of choosing between paths that would not only define the end of her investigation, but also the course of her own ethics in a tangled and confusing world.

Chapter 14

Obscured
Revelations

Amid the chaos and uncertainty, shocking revelations about the very origin of the memories, which had long been kept hidden in the shadows, began to emerge. The very foundations of the underground market were shaking as dark truths came to light, defying everything they thought they knew.

In the midst of this whirlwind of discovery, Leah was in the eye of the storm. Each revelation shattered her foundations of what she thought she knew about the souvenir market. Deep secrets, buried under layers of deceit and silence, now stood as pillars supporting a truth that had been concealed with extreme care. Each new revelation was like a flash of light illuminating a previously dark and masked world.

Leah discovered a bleak truth that revealed intense manipulation in the creation and trade of memories. Behind the secret exchanges and obscure transactions, a complex web of influences emerged that went back to the very origins of the memories that were being bought and sold.

Every memory, every experience, was intertwined with hidden threads that stretched into a past full of intrigue and machinations.

The memories Leah delved into revealed a haunting truth: they weren't mere recollections but intricately constructed illusions. It struck her like a thunderbolt that these memories weren't pristine reflections of reality but crafted, twisted, or even implanted, betraying the very essence of truth. It was as if someone had tampered with the canvas of life, painting falsehoods into the most intimate moments of people's existence. Discovering this manipulation was like stumbling upon a hidden maze where every corner held a distorted narrative.

Her dismay knew no bounds as she peeled back the layers of these falsified memories. It felt like witnessing a masterpiece tainted by forgeries.

The shock was palpable, realizing that moments once believed genuine were nothing more than elaborate fabrications. It tore at the fabric of trust, leaving behind a trail of doubt that eclipsed the authenticity of every memory she encountered. The realization hit like a tidal wave, shaking the very core of her belief in the purity of memories.

These revelations struck Leah like an earthquake. The realization that someone had manipulated the very essence of human experiences was like discovering a breach in the sanctity of life itself. The gravity of this discovery wasn't just about fabricated recollections; it undermined the integrity of existence. It was a disconcerting dance with a reality where truth and authenticity blurred, leaving her grappling with the moral implications of this deceitful intrusion into people's lives.

The seismic revelation shook the core of the underground market, shattering the illusion of authenticity that once adorned every memory.

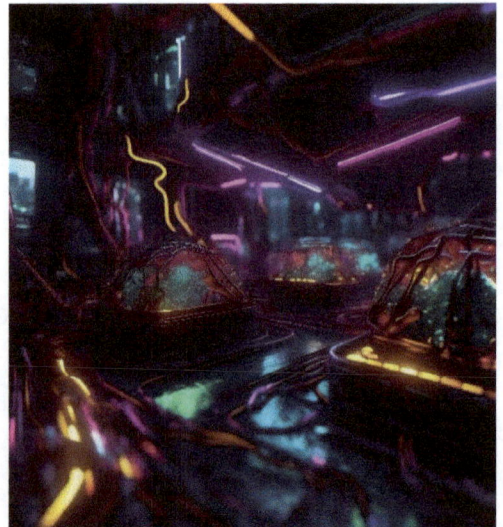

What was once a sanctuary for genuine recollections now stood clouded by an unsettling truth: the memories were tainted. The market, a beacon of nostalgia and heartfelt moments, transformed into a labyrinth of doubts and disillusionment. It was akin to unraveling a cherished tapestry only to discover it was woven with threads of deception and manipulation.

The market's essence shifted drastically. What were once prized possessions, cherished as glimpses into the past, became suspect. The air crackled with uncertainty as patrons reevaluated the very essence of their treasured memories. It was a collective jolt, as if the ground beneath their feet had shifted, leaving them uncertain about the genuineness of every shared moment. The once-vibrant marketplace now echoed with whispers of doubt, casting shadows on the sanctity of every memory up for trade.

The reverberations of this revelation were felt far and wide. Trust, once the cornerstone of the marketplace, fractured.

It was as if a veil had been lifted, revealing a disconcerting reality: the memories they held dear were not immune to manipulation. The very soul of the market, built on the authenticity of shared experiences, faced a moment of reckoning. Every whispered conversation, every exchanged memory, now carried an air of suspicion. It was a profound shift, a turning point where the market's core values clashed with a newfound, uncomfortable truth.

Instead of bringing clarity, they generated a whirlwind of doubts. Could they trust what seemed authentic? The revelations shook the foundations of the market, challenging the trust placed in those who ran it. The integrity of the entire system was at stake, and each new revelation tarnished the image of what was once considered a safe and authentic space.

The decisions she had to make resonated with the fate of the underground market and, perhaps, the very fabric of society that rested on it. Responsibility weighed heavily on her shoulders, each election carrying the weight of a potential redefinition of future course.

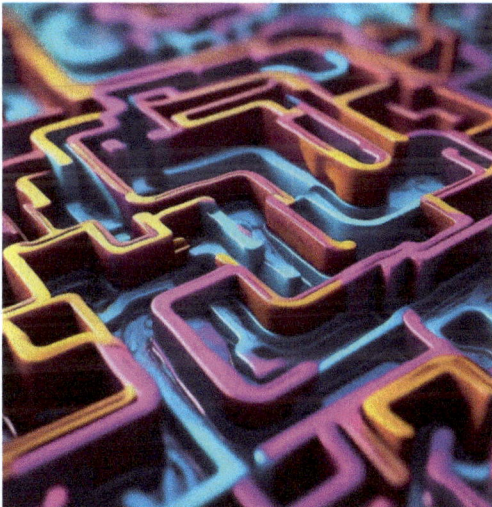

Chapter 15

The Enemy
Revealed

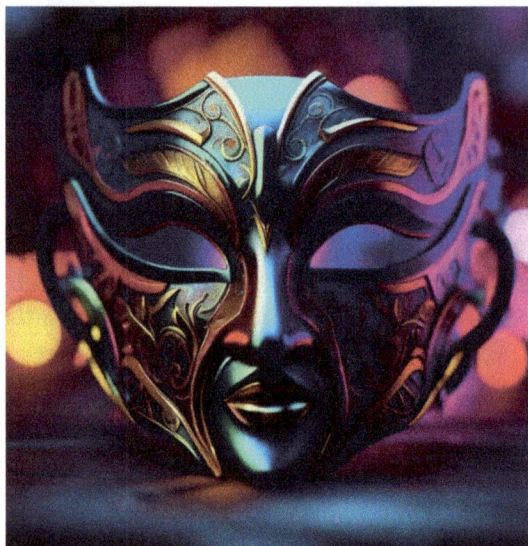

The mystery surrounding the Merchant of Instants vanished like mist at dawn, revealing the figure hidden behind the veil. For Leah and her allie, that revelation was like a gust of wind, taking with it a whirlwind of surprise and revelations. They came face-to-face with the person behind the mysterious mask, an encounter that set off a rollercoaster of unexpected emotions and truths.

The revelation of who the Merchant really was was like an earthquake in the world they had been exploring. Surprise and disbelief mingled in a whirlwind of emotions when the mask was finally removed and the real culprit behind the whole occult market network was revealed. It was as if everything they thought they knew was shaken, leaving them stunned and shocked.

Leah's eyes widened in stunned realization as she locked gazes with the enigmatic figure before her. The Merchant of Instants stood there, no longer an elusive enigma, but a startlingly familiar presence. It was a moment of startling recognition, an unexpected convergence of paths that she never foresaw. The revelation struck her like a bolt of lightning, unraveling the threads of secrecy that had cloaked the Merchant's identity.

As the truth dawned upon her, a whirlwind of emotions swept through Leah. The realization that the Merchant was someone intimately intertwined with her life sent ripples of astonishment through her. Every shared memory, every interaction she had with this figure, now took on a new, perplexing meaning. It was as if a veil had been lifted, revealing a profound connection she had never fathomed. The familiarity in the Merchant's eyes echoed an unspoken history, an uncharted territory of shared experiences. Leah found herself grappling with a flood of questions, each one unraveling a piece of this puzzling revelation. How had their paths intertwined in such clandestine ways? What hidden narratives lurked beneath the surface of their encounters? It was a juncture where the past, present, and the mysterious figure of the Merchant converged, entwined in a tapestry of enigmatic truths.

The newly revealed identity defied all her understanding, unearthing unexpected connections that resonated in her most difficult moments. It was as if the veil had been lifted, showing her a totally new and unknown panorama.

The revelation about who the enemy really was uncovered a tapestry of deception and manipulation that had spread over time. Hidden secrets and clandestine alliances were now revealed in a new light, completely transforming the perception of all involved in this intricate web.

It was as if they had discovered a set of connections that were previously hidden, altering their view of everything they had believed until then.

The discovery of who the Merchant was resonated not only with Leah and her allie, but also unleashed a barrage of revelations that shook the boundaries of trust and truth. The Merchant's revealed identity was not only the pinnacle of her search for answers, but unleashed a new gale of questions and challenges.

It was as if every piece of certainty had been moved, shaking the foundations of what they thought they knew. Doubts multiplied and confrontation with the truth became more crucial than ever.

At that very moment when the veil of mystery was falling, a new strife broke out, a struggle that transcended the merely physical to enter the realms of the hear.

The revelation of who the enemy was a complete game-changer, opening the way for a confrontation that would not only be a test of strength, but also an examination of loyalties and deep convictions. It was as if the battlefield was transformed into a field of decisions, where every move became crucial, not only because of what it meant in the fight, but because of the weight it had on one's integrity and on the most deeply held values.

Chapter 16

Race Against Time

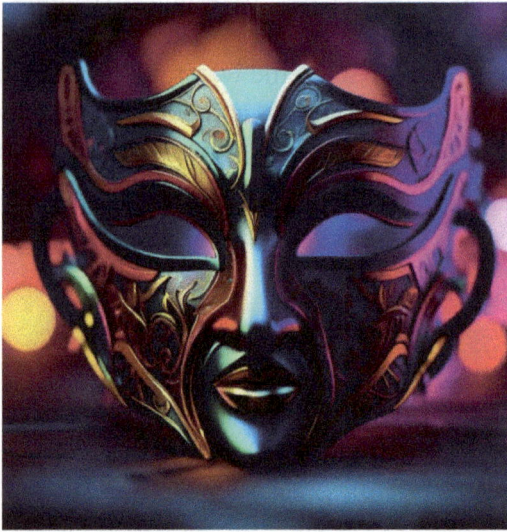

In the midst of an underground market that hung on a tightrope, the ticking of the clock became an incessant reminder of an ever-narrowing boundary. Leah and herallie were in a race against time, locked in a frenzied race against time, determined to dismantle this shadowy web before the repercussions became catastrophic and absolutely irreparable. Every second was vital, every move meant the difference between safeguarding or falling a universe of secrets.

NeoMind, the very foundations of the dark market were beginning to shake. The Merchant of Instants, now revealed in his identity, redoubled his efforts to maintain control, but each maneuver of his was like an added link in the chain that inexorably brought him closer to his ultimate revelation. Every action, every movement, became one more thread on the intricate path that led to its final unmasking.

Leah and her companion moved steadily forward, joining forces and facing challenges as they explored the darkest corners of the secret market. Every step they took was vital, every election became a turning point in this unbridled race to disrupt the network that had exerted their control for a long period.

Every strategy was calculated, every move measured with precision, aware that every decision could be the key to dismantling the clandestine network.

Time slipped away like grains of sand on a broken clock, and the urge to act became almost unbearable. Every minute that passed was one more step towards the edge of an abyss, a constant reminder of the need to end this tangled web of deception and concealment before the effects were irreparable. Every second was like the beat of a drum, an urgent call to unravel this mystery before it was too late.

The determination of Leah and her allie was fueled by the sense of urgency that enveloped every action. There was no room for mistakes, every decision had to be precise and accurate, every move calculated with precision to dismantle this web of betrayals and deceptions.

The implications of this race against the clock were enormous, like the weight of a building on fragile shoulders. It wasn't just about dismantling that market hidden in the shadows, it was like weaving a web of protection around broken lives.

Lives were intertwined with manipulated memories, their threads stretched like cobwebs in a storm, and time ran mercilessly, squeezing its pace. The urgency wasn't just about ending the obscure exchange of memories, it was about rescuing the very essence of those whose souls had been used as currency in this twisted game.

Every moment that passed was a drop in the ocean of devastating possibilities that could be unleashed if the delay persisted: fragments of fractured identities, shattered hopes, and a continuous flow of suffering in an already violated world. It was more than a battle against time, it was a struggle to give back what had been taken from them: the dignity, integrity, and freedom of those whose destinies had been manipulated by the whims of this underground market.

Between the deafening chaos and the simmering pressure, Leah and her allie moved like pieces of a puzzle, each with their crucial role in this journey. Every step, every move, was like adding a vital piece to complete the mosaic of this confrontation. The clock, like an implacable judge, ticked down constantly, reminding them that every second lost brought the underground market closer to a precipice from which there was no return.

The need to act quickly and decisively hung over them, like an implacable shadow that threatened to plunge them into an abyss of uncontrollable consequences if they did not manage to close the curtain on this dark drama in time. Every gesture, every choice, became a link in the chain that would decide the fate of many, pushing them towards the climax of this crossroads where time was the greatest enemy.

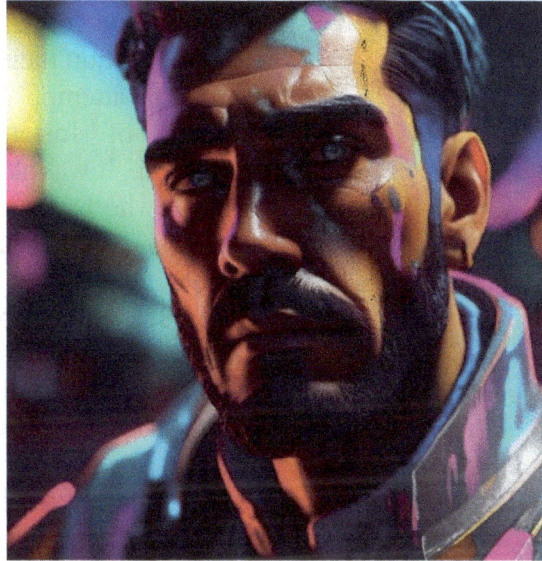

Chapter 17

The Last Offer

At the culmination of the final battle against the underground market, when the denouement was looming on the horizon, a tempting offer rose as a challenge to the morality of Leah and her companion. An unexpected proposal, laden with tantalizing and dangerous promises, threatened to undermine the foundations of their struggle and call into question their deepest convictions.

In a final attempt to uphold his control, the Merchant of Instants dangled a tantalizing proposition.. It was akin to a test of moral fortitude for those who had staunchly held their ground, a temptation that whispered convenience and immediate gain. This offer, draped in an enticing façade, seemed to promise an easier path, a shortcut through the tangled web of complexities. Yet, beneath its appealing surface, it bore the same murky shadows and twisted machinations that had defined its presence since inception. For some of them, it was a test of resilience, a challenge to the very principles they clung to. The Merchant's proposal dangled like a tempting fruit, promising to ease the burdens of the tumultuous journey. Yet, lurking beneath its surface, lay the unsettling echoes of past deceptions and hidden agendas. It was an offer that blurred the lines between necessity and compromise, entreating a crossroads of moral dilemmas.

The Merchant's offer whispered promises of an easier path, promising solace in a tumultuous landscape. It was an invitation fraught with allure, a subtle seduction that tested the resolve of those weary from the unrelenting storm. The temptation to accept, to yield to the allure of ease, tugged at the very fabric of their convictions. But beneath the surface of this seemingly benevolent proposition lay the lingering shadows of uncertainty and doubt, a cautionary reminder of the dangers lurking within its seemingly golden veneer.

Amidst the mounting tension, the proposal emerged as a gauntlet thrown down to those who had tirelessly combated the shadows of deceit. It served as a final, calculated ploy, a tactical move to probe the resilience of their beliefs and commitments. This proposition, like a fork in the road, presented an ethical quandary where expediency and steadfast principles clashed headlong. It sought to sow seeds of doubt, an insidious whisper that sought to erode the very bedrock of their steadfastness, cunningly orchestrated as the Merchant's ultimate test of their resolve.

The proposal loomed large, casting a shadow over the unwavering defenders of truth and authenticity. It was a strategic maneuver, a calculated move aimed to sway the staunch guardians of morality. This offer, a subtle challenge, invited them to question the very fiber of their convictions, to deliberate over the trade-off between convenience and unwavering integrity.

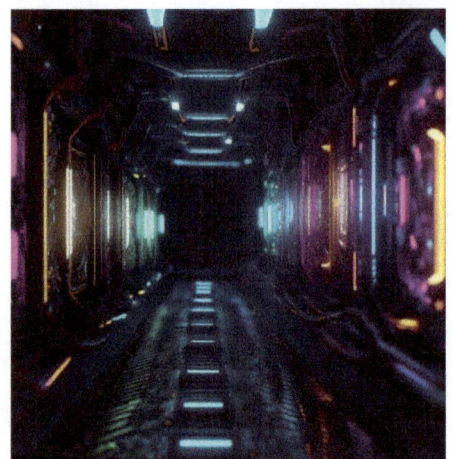

The Merchant's gambit played out as a pivotal moment, where their unwavering stance faced the ultimate test against the allure of a seemingly simpler path.

The proposal glimmered like a lone beacon in the midst of the tumultuous storm. It posed a formidable test to the moral fortitude of those who had been resolute in their quest for truth.

This enticement, cunningly designed, posed a critical crossroads where steadfast principles danced on the edge of compromise. It was an invitation to reconsider the unyielding stance, dangling the illusion of an easier route in a landscape fraught with moral complexities. Yet, amidst this calculated ploy, lay the undeniable truth of its intrinsic shadows, beckoning them to hold firm against the allure of the Merchant's final gambit. The offer glow, as if it was a magic key to solve everything easily and smoothly.

It was like a promising escape door, a way out that ensured stopping the imminent collapse of the underground market without sacrificing much. However, that easy way out came with a hidden price, conditions that bordered a blurred line between what was right and what seemed convenient.

A tempting promise wrapped in shiny packaging but full of pitfalls and ethical dilemmas, a shortcut that seemed easy but challenged the integrity of those who were determined to eradicate the darkness that shrouded this market.

In the tapestry of possibilities, the proposal shimmered like a gleaming gem, offering the allure of stability and order in the tumultuous landscape. It dangled the promise of immediate resolution, a swift remedy to quell the storm that had roiled their world. Yet, behind its tempting facade lay a deeper riddle—a test not just of their choices, but of the very essence of their fight.

The allure of a shortcut, while promising to sidestep prolonged turmoil, begged the question: at what price would such immediate respite come? It posed a conundrum that threatened to undercut the core purpose that had initially ignited their quest.

The proposal stood as a beacon of momentary relief in the chaos, a mirage of control and stability in the ever-shifting sands of uncertainty. It was a seductive siren song, promising a swift exit from the turbulence that had ensnared them. Yet, buried beneath its surface allure was a weighty dilemma that probed the heart of their cause. The temptation of a shortcut offered the chance to circumvent prolonged strife, but at the steep cost of forsaking the very principles that had propelled their journey. It was an offer wrapped in paradox—a resolution that could simultaneously bring order while undermining the fundamental ethos that had driven their collective mission.

The proposal beckoned with the promise of calm amid the storm, a potential reprieve from the chaos that had beset their endeavors. Its allure lay in its guise of swift resolution, a seemingly convenient solution to the labyrinthine problems they faced. Yet, within its tempting veneer lurked a crucial test, an examination of the very core of their struggle. The allure of a shortcut seemed to offer an escape from prolonged turmoil, but it posed a grave trade-off—a relinquishment of the principles and values that had fueled their relentless pursuit. It was a challenge not just to their choices, but to the very essence of their unwavering commitment to truth and authenticity.

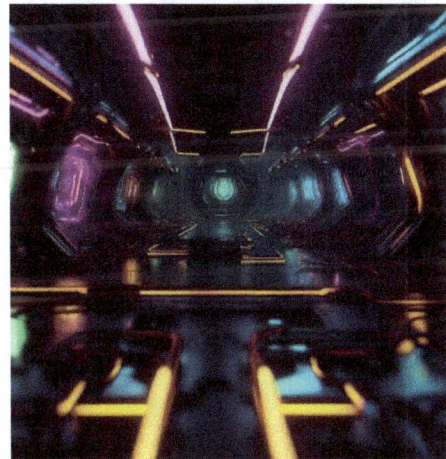

The tension between what was seen as a quick resolution and the convictions that had guided them up to that point generated a storm of doubt and deep reflections on the true meaning of their battle and the implications of taking a shortcut to an uncertain outcome.

At the crossroads between ethics and expediency, became blurred, dissolved into a scenario full of tantalizing possibilities and inevitable sacrifices. That offer, more than a simple solution to stop the imminent collapse of the underground market, represented a direct challenge to the values and convictions that had been the driving force of Leah and her companionn on this exhausting journey. It was like being at the epicenter of a storm, where the promise of stability collided head-on with integrity, testing every fiber of their being and forcing them to question the true cost of taking the fastest path.

At this critical point, the decision they had to make would not only influence the outcome of their struggle, but also the legacy they would leave behind. The final proposal placed them at a crossroads between comfort and integrity, a dilemma that forced them to confront the true meaning of their cause. They were on the threshold of final resolution, where the integrity of their convictions and the very essence of their struggle were brought to a final judgment at this crucial stage of the battle.

Chapter 18

The Battle in
the Shadows

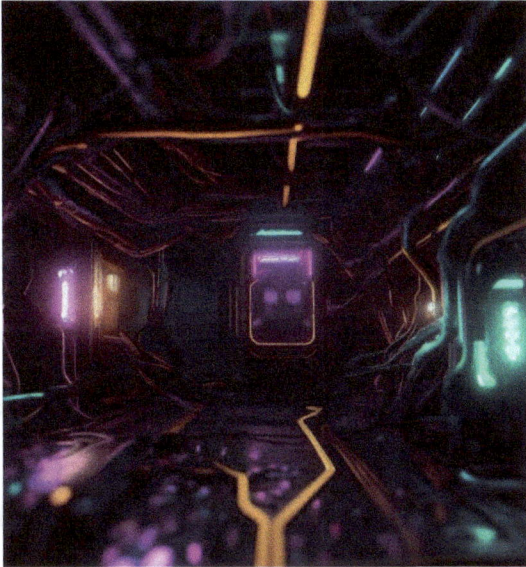

Amid the darkness and uncertainty, the ultimate confrontation erupted between two opposing fronts: those fighting to destroy the underground market and those determined to maintain their influence and power.

An epic battle ensued, plunging NeoMind into a titanic struggle between forces seeking annihilation and those resisting its dismantling.

Leah and her companion were lined up in a chaotic challenge, a kind of messy dance of strategies and tactics. On the one hand, there were them, determined to unravel the ins and outs of an underground market that had hidden secrets for far too long.

On the other side, there were those bent on maintaining the shadows, fervent in their mission to preserve a dark status quo.

Strategic decisions reverberated around every corner of NeoMind, every move marking a step forward in the battle. Leah and her allie, driven by the conviction to bring the hidden truth to light, were faced with an equally determined force. The conflict wasn't just physical; It was imbued with tension and determination of two worlds at odds. It was a struggle between those who sought to dismantle a nefarious system and those willing to protect it at any cost.

Each encounter was a crossroads between the search for truth and the defense of a system rooted in darkness. The resistance to every move by Leah and her companion revealed the tenacity of those who defended the underground market, a fierce effort to maintain control of something that remained hidden from the eyes of society. The challenges were constant: strategies intertwined with tactics entangled with ethics, all while the pulse of confrontation echoed in every corner of the city.

In every calculated move, a grand struggle of ideologies played out, transcending the mere dismantling of an underground market. It evolved into a clash of principles, a monumental duel pitting the unwavering virtues of integrity and justice against the pervasive forces of corruption and deceit. The battlefield was not merely physical but ideological—a battleground where the very essence of moral rectitude and righteousness grappled against the treacherous undercurrents of falsehood and malfeasance.

Each tactical maneuver became a testament to a broader conflict, transcending the realm of a mere commercial battle. It burgeoned into an ideological showdown, where the forces advocating for righteousness and principled conduct clashed vehemently against the dark currents of dishonesty and malpractice. It wasn't just about dismantling a market; it was a cosmic collision between the unwavering standards of integrity and the insidious tendrils of corruption, a struggle for the moral compass that guided NeoMind's fate.

Every strategic choice bore the weight of a conflict that surpassed the tangible battles. It escalated beyond the confines of a market's dismantlement, evolving into a battle for moral ascendancy. It was the collision of values against the backdrop of systemic corruption—a strife where the relentless pursuit of justice and the sanctity

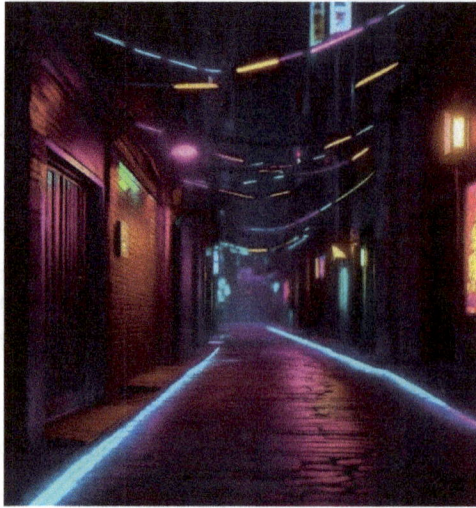

of principles locked horns with the pervasive tendrils of deceit and malfeasance. The struggle wasn't solely about erasing an underground market; it was a profound ideological confrontation for the very soul and integrity of NeoMind.

The confrontation was not only a contest of forces, but a test of deep-rooted values on each side. On the one hand, there was Leah and her allie, committed to revealing the truth, ready to unravel corruption and restore justice. On the other, those who clung to the darkness of the underground market, determined to maintain a system that hovered over the truth.

Each strategic move was a reflection of truth versus lies, integrity versus manipulation. The confrontation resonated not only on the battlefields, but in the dilemma of values that defined each of those involved. It was a struggle for the very soul of NeoMind, a battle that went beyond the physical.

The dark alleys of NeoMind became the epicenter of a contest that went beyond simple physical confrontations. That confrontation not only involved forces confronting each other directly, but also reflected the inner struggle of those dedicated to the cause. Each blow, each strategy deployed, not only sought to unbalance the adversary, but also to achieve a victory that transcended the merely visible.

The alleys, usually dark and forgotten, became the scene of a duel that reflected the clashes of ideologies, passions and deep convictions.Every step taken in those labyrinths nooks and crannies was not only a physical breakthrough, but a display of determination and inner strength. It was a struggle that was sustained on the edge of one's convictions, a conflict where strategies materialized not only in attacks, but in resistance in the face of temptation and doubt.

The shadows of those alleys harbored a battle that reflected the confrontation between the obvious and the underlying. Every strategic move was the product of an internal struggle, the manifestation of perseverance in the face of adversity. It was a dance of physical and mental prowess, where tactics were not only based on physical attacks, but on resistance to the temptation to give in to the pressure of the adversary.

The dark corners of NeoMind became the battleground for a struggle that embodied the clash of visible and invisible forces.

Every action, every strategy, was the result of an internal conflict, a battle not only for physical supremacy, but for resistance to external influences. It was a confrontation that extended beyond blows, a contest marked by firmness of character and the internal struggle to remain true to values and convictions.

The titanic clash between forces in the darkness marked a crucial turning point in NeoMind's history. The contest, unbridled and charged with meaning, reflected the colossal weight of every decision and action that had shaped that climactic moment. It was a moment where the very fate of an entire society hung on the outcome of that epic confrontation.

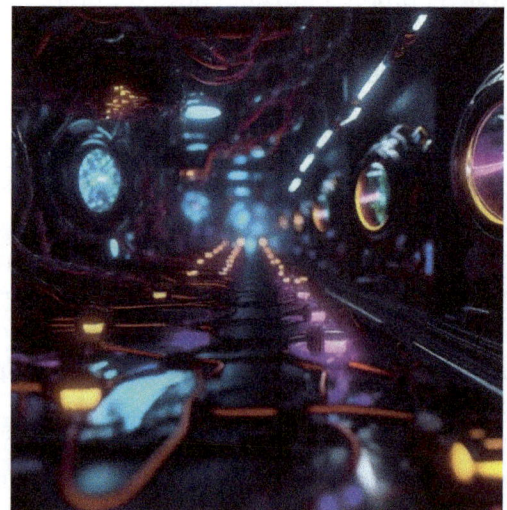

It was an unprecedented showdown, a clash of wills and strategies that reverberated throughout NeoMind's history. Each movement represented a transcendental chapter, where the weight of previous actions converged in a collision of monumental proportions.

The outcome would not only define the fate of those involved, but also the very course of the society that inhabited that universe.

The battle embodied the zenith of a narrative woven with the decisions and actions of each individual in NeoMind. It was a turning point, where the intensity of each blow, each strategy deployed, resounded like an echo of the past, present and future of that society. Each side fought not only for victory on the battlefield, but for the influence that would determine the future of their world.

It was a high point where the threads of fate converged. The conflict, fraught with meaning and transcendence, represented an epic moment in which the collective weight of every past decision came to life. The very future of NeoMind hung in the balance, awaiting the outcome of this monumental confrontation that would determine the course of its history.

Each side, with its deep-rooted motivations, was determined to defend its ideals, hoping to secure the fate of the underground market, whose shadows hung across the city.

Chapter 19

The Price of Exchange

After the cataclysm that marked the end of the underground market, the aftermath spread like long shadows over NeoMind. The dismantling of this dark web not only left a tangible void in the urban fabric, but also unleashed a number of unexpected side effects and ushered in a relentless transformation in the life of the city and its residents.

The repercussions of this rupture reverberated through every alley, every corner, affecting the dynamics of the city in unforeseen ways. The demise of the underground market left behind a void that expanded like an open wound, transforming urban landscapes and daily routines. The city, once permeated by the shadows of this clandestine network, now faced a new scenario, one where social and economic dynamics were faltering in search of a new equilibrium.

The dissolution of the underground market had far-reaching effects, etching emotional imprints on the very souls of NeoMind's inhabitants. The city bore witness to a seismic shift in the fabric of reality, ushering in an era shrouded in ambiguity and trepidation. The once-assured understanding of what constituted truth and authenticity had been cast into doubt.

Relationships that had been interwoven by the undercurrents of the clandestine market found themselves in a state of disarray. The bonds between citizens, once forged in the crucible of these shadowy dealings, now stood in need of reconstruction.

The city's inhabitants embarked on a collective journey to mend the fractures that had eroded trust and integrity, endeavoring to rebuild the foundations of their connections on a new, more genuine footing.

Moreover, the aftermath of the underground market's demise weighed heavily on the emotional landscape of NeoMind.

The echoes of its collapse reverberated in the hearts of its denizens, imprinting a profound sense of disillusionment and vulnerability. The very essence of truth had been called into question, instilling a pervasive sense of wariness and caution in the once-assured perspectives of the city's inhabitants.

As they navigated this uncertain terrain, they sought to reconcile the fractures in their perceptions, endeavoring to redefine their understanding of trust and authenticity in a world irrevocably altered by the market's demise.

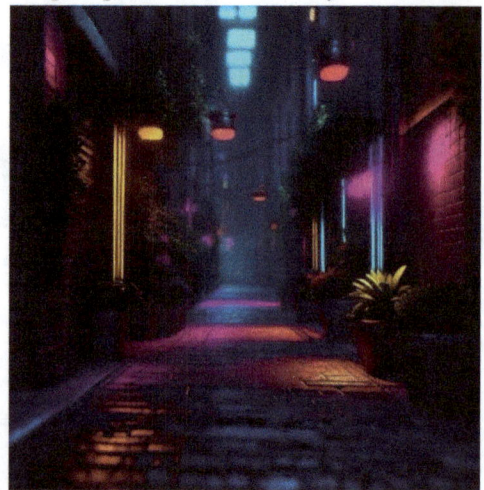

The unfolding of unintended consequences and the transformation of the city generated a period of readjustment, a turbulent transition to an uncertain future. The dismantling of the underground market marked a turning point in the history of NeoMind, altering its essence and challenging its inhabitants to rebuild their reality on the foundations of truth and transparency.

The traces left by this titanic struggle spread like fractures throughout the city, revealing the true dimension of the cost paid in pursuit of truth and justice. The cracks became a visible symbol of transformation, marking not only the demise of this underground market, but also

the consequences it left in its wake. On every corner, on every building, the scars bore witness to the battle that took place in the shadows. The city, once influenced by the machinations of the dark market, was now facing a period of redefinition and restructuring.

The mixed emotions of relief and concern were intertwined in the hearts of those who had witnessed the dismantling of this clandestine network. The lives of citizens, once woven together by the invisible threads of this hidden market, were now faced with the task of rebuilding lost trust and social bonds.

The demise of the underground market created a vacuum in NeoMind's economy and social structure. Business dynamics and social interactions, once shaped by the influences of this dark web, were reorganized in search of a new equilibrium. The closure of this network had a domino effect in different sectors of the city, generating a period of adaptation and adjustment that marked the beginning of an era of change and evolution.

The underground market's dissolution manifested vividly in the lives of those entangled within its enigmatic web. The voids left by the absence of genuine memories or the alteration of their essence cast a heavy pall over those who had once been part of this clandestine network. Their existence, formerly sculpted by these manipulated recollections, now existed within an unrelenting labyrinth of uncertainty and internal discord.

Evidences of these emotional burdens painted a poignant narrative across their countenances.

Faces etched with the residue of lost or tainted memories reflected a poignant tale of inner turmoil and unspoken sorrow. Their distant gazes spoke volumes, haunted by echoes of moments distorted or erased, while each weary sigh carried the weight of a soul grappling with the fractures of its own narrative. In these silent gestures, an entire saga of anguish and introspection unfolded, a testament to the profound impact of tampered memories on the very fabric of their beings.

They had been stripped of fragments of their own history, fragments that had given them identity and meaning. Now, in the midst of uncertainty, they struggled to rebuild themselves, to reconcile the discrepancy between the reality they knew and the truth emerging through the cracks of their memories.

The search for identity became an emotional odyssey, a journey full of challenges and unanswered questions.How do they reconstruct what has been faded or distorted? How can they reconcile the present with the fragments of a past that now seemed confused and distant?.They were immersed in a process of rediscovery, trying to link scattered fragments together to create a coherent narrative about who they really were.

Grief and confusion intertwined in their lives, forming a complex web of emotions. Despite the will to move forward, they faced constant challenges to understand their own history, to reconstruct their identities torn by the threads of an underground market that had altered the course of their existences.

The very essence of NeoMind, a city where memories used to be the currency, was in the midst of a radical metamorphosis. The transformation had unleashed a storm of emotions and changes that reverberated through every corner of the city.

The atmosphere that had once been steeped in nostalgia and echoes of the past now swayed between the hope of a new beginning and the immense weight of faded memories.

The streets vibrated with a different energy, tinged with uncertainty and wonder. People, once connected through shared experiences, now looked at each other with eyes laden with doubts and suspicions. Relationships that once flourished in mutual trust were challenged, entangled in threads of uncertainty and fear of the unknown.

The social fabric of NeoMind was being reconfigured. The bonds that used to bind the community were now disrupted, transformed by the absence of shared memories. The entire city was torn between two worlds: one that promised freedom from the bonds of the past and another that mourned the loss of a unique connection that once defined collective identity. The duality of emotions hung in the air, painting a landscape of change, but also of nostalgia and adaptation.

The fall of the underground market not only marked the end of an era, but left behind a trail of unforeseen consequences and an ocean of doubts flooding society's thoughts. Victory in the battle had been achieved, yet its price was far higher than anyone had anticipated.

The void left by the disappearance of this illicit market was palpable in every corner of the city. Although the dark web had been dismantled, its impact resonated as a lingering echo in the collective psyche of society. The population was torn between a sense of relief at the end of a murky chapter and uneasiness about the unknown consequences that awaited on the horizon.

The streets, once populated by secret transactions and clandestine meetings, now seemed to be plunged into an unusual silence. However, this silence was not an indicator of peace, but rather a reflection of the confusion and uneasiness that gripped the minds of the inhabitants.

Unanswered questions and the shadow of the past hung over the city, creating an atmosphere of uncertainty that hindered the feeling of triumph for having overthrown a corrupt system.

Leah and her companion, who had forged a sacrificial path for the truth, were at an emotional crossroads. The victory they had achieved brought with it a mixture of mixed emotions. Despite the satisfaction of having defeated the dark underground market, a bittersweet feeling gripped them.

Triumph was mixed with a feeling of introspection and reflection. As they contemplated the fruits of their struggle, they also faced the weight of the consequences.

Decisions made in the heat of battle now presented themselves as question marks, questioning whether the cost paid had been justified by the cause they defended. The desire for truth and justice clashed with doubts about whether the price of victory had been worth it in terms of the personal and social repercussions that unfolded before them.

The transformed lives, altered memories, and fractured relationships were tangible proof that the search for truth, though noble, had left its indelible mark on the city and the lives of its inhabitants.

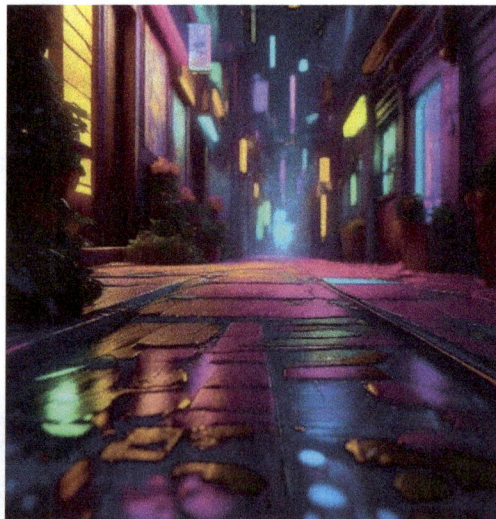

Chapter 20

The Denouement

At the very moment when the city was still throbbing with the echoes of battle, Leah was at the epicenter of a discovery as moving as it was heartbreaking about the essence of memories. As NeoMind struggled between healing the deep wounds caused by greed and seeking redemption. She was confronted with a truth whose magnitude could alter the course not only of her life, but also of all those affected by the relentless struggle against the underground market.

The city, became the scene of a renaissance and a struggle for emotional reconstruction. In the midst of this whirlwind of newfound emotions and realities. At the climactic moment of revelations, Leah immersed herself in a deeply moving understanding. She discovered that memories were not just fragments stored in the mind, but pieces of authenticity that went beyond any transaction or manipulation.

In every recollection, Leah delved beyond the surface, sensing the authenticity interwoven within the vivid experiences and emotions encapsulated in those memories. Each fragment of the past wasn't just a moment frozen in time; it was an invaluable treasure trove, carrying the weight of genuine feelings and stories. These weren't mere commodities for exchange; they were the embodiment of human existence—a profound tapestry that resonated with the essence of joy, pain, love, and resilience.

The impact of these genuine memories transcended the confines of the material world. They held a mysterious power, an inexplicable force that transcended the tangible. These memories weren't just snapshots of a bygone era; they were the living essence of humanity. They had the capability to bridge rifts, heal deep-seated wounds, and bind together the fragmented souls of NeoMind that had been rattled by discord and deceit.

For Leah, the realization wasn't merely an intellectual grasp of the situation; it was an emotional revelation. It dawned upon her that these authentic memories were more than historical records—they were catalysts for transformation. Each genuine memory held within it the potential to ignite hope, repair shattered trust, and rebuild the city's fractured spirit. They were beacons of light, illuminating the way toward a NeoMind where honesty, empathy, and authenticity could thrive once

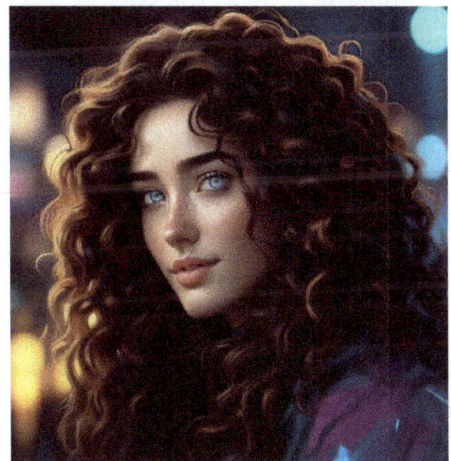

more. Leah embarked on a new expedition, fueled by an unyielding resolve and armed with the invaluable revelations she had acquired. Her determination carved a path toward a singular goal: the reunification of a fractured city, guided by the beacon of authentic memories as her most trusted ally.

With unwavering commitment, Leah dedicated herself wholeheartedly to the cause, channeling every ounce of her being into the endeavor of healing the torn fabric of NeoMind. Each genuine memory she unearthed became a potent instrument, akin to a healing balm, meticulously applied to the collective wounds festering within the city's soul. She toiled tirelessly, navigating the intricate landscape of memories, delicately orchestrating a symphony of authenticity in a world once clouded by deceit. For Leah, every authentic recollection held the

potential to bridge divides, mend broken spirits, and stitch together the fragmented essence of NeoMind.

In Leah's hands, these authentic memories became the cornerstone of her mission to rebuild fractured trust and nurture unity within the city's populace. She meticulously wove these threads of authenticity into the very fabric of NeoMind, countering the looming shadows cast by greed and deceit.

Every memory, like a shimmering beacon, held the promise of a better tomorrow. They served as catalysts for rekindling lost trust, sparking conversations, and fostering a newfound sense of solidarity among the inhabitants.

Leah wielded these memories not just as fragments of the past, but as tools to illuminate a path toward renewal, healing, and a harmonious future.

With each memory restored to its unaltered truth, Leah sowed the seeds of a collective narrative, one that was free from manipulation and deception. These memories acted as testaments to the authenticity and resilience of the city, forming the foundation upon which the renewed NeoMind could rise, united in its shared history and aspirations.

Leah's dedication to NeoMind's restoration unveiled a dual journey—one of personal reckoning intertwined with the city's collective redemption. Her pursuit of healing echoed a deeper, individual quest for absolution. With every effort made to mend the fractured memories of the city, she found herself on a parallel path, confronting her own history.

As Leah delved deeper into the restoration process, she faced her past with a newfound clarity.

Her endeavor to restore truth and authenticity within NeoMind mirrored her own pursuit of honesty and integrity. Each genuine memory she resurrected was a mirror reflecting, her own convictions, emphasizing the intrinsic value of truth in her life.

In the process of healing the city's wounds, Leah found herself reconciling with her own experiences. The act of repairing NeoMind's collective memory became a catalyst for her personal journey, prompting introspection and a profound realization of the significance of veracity and honesty within herself.

Every smile that graced the faces of NeoMind's inhabitants symbolized more than just a return of lost memories; it mirrored Leah's personal journey towards reconciliation. Each embrace that eased emotional burdens was a testament to her own healing amidst the turmoil that had rattled not only her life but the very essence of the city itself.

In her efforts to mend the collective soul of NeoMind, she found solace and redemption, intertwining her personal story with that of the city.

As the echoes of the final battle faded, NeoMind stood not only as a theater of triumph but as a canvas awaiting a new masterpiece. The aftermath of conflict served as the fertile ground for a fresh beginning. The city's horizon stretched wide open, beckoning the brushstrokes of a revitalized era, where authenticity and truth would be the vibrant hues painting its future.

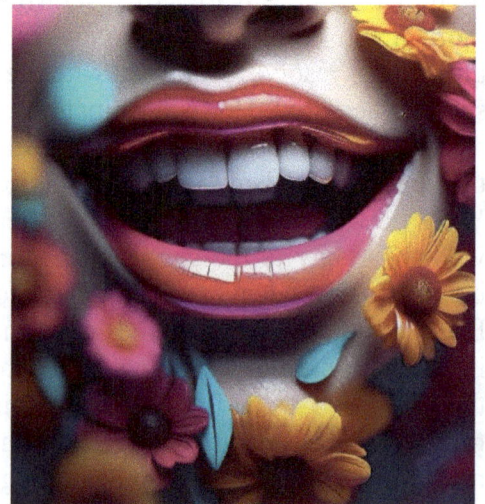

The streets, once steeped in the shadows of deception and manipulation, now witnessed the dawn of a different narrative. Each step, each gesture of restoration, and every shared memory became strokes on this blank canvas, outlining a narrative of unity and healing. The city was in a transformative state, not just recovering from its wounds but embracing a newfound identity steeped in honesty and solidarity.

Leah emerged as the beacon of this renaissance. Her every move echoed a steadfast commitment to crafting a future anchored in the ideals of truth and

authenticity. She envisioned a society reshaped by these values, where the past served as a testament to resilience rather than a breeding ground for manipulation.

With each stride forward, Leah laid the groundwork for a transformed future. Her vision was not just to mend the past but to construct a new beginning, where the threads of authenticity would weave a tapestry of trust and unity among the inhabitants of NeoMind.

Leah's determination to forge this path was unwavering. She saw beyond the scars of the city, envisioning a tomorrow built on the solid bedrock of genuine memories. Her actions spoke of a leader committed to cultivating an environment where the truth would flourish, nurturing a community founded on trust and unadulterated experiences.

With every step, they rewrote the narrative of authenticity, stitching threads of truth into the tapestry of the city's collective consciousness. Authentic memories no longer just represented the past; they became a beacon guiding a community yearning for a future founded on honesty and trust.

Their commitment went beyond repairing the damages caused by the manipulation of memories. They cultivated a cultural shift—a societal transformation that breathed life into the once obscured, now genuine, memories. These memories weren't just snapshots of history but the seeds of a new ethos, fostering an environment where transparency and integrity thrived.

Their influence was like a ripple that traversed the city's pulse, pulsating through conversations held in cozy cafes, street corners, and marketplaces.

Every genuine memory acted not just as a snapshot but as a vivid testament, each recollection symbolized a victory, a marker on the path toward reinstating a culture of trust and authenticity.

Rectifying past manipulations was just the beginning—a precursor to something more profound. It was a deliberate act of planting seeds of courage in the hearts of every citizen, a collective endeavor to craft a future where truth and hope prevailed.

Their impact wasn't confined to grand gestures but was felt in the simplicity of everyday life. It seeped into the mundane, making honesty and transparency commonplace virtues. Each conversation echoed their dedication, subtly urging individuals to embrace authenticity and contribute to a society where integrity was no longer a rarity but a guiding principle. It was a call to action, encouraging everyone to become ambassadors of truth, weaving their narratives into the city's evolving tapestry of honesty and hope.

Their vision wasn't merely to rectify the wrongs but to sculpt a collective consciousness where every authentic memory was a testament to the triumph of honesty.

It was an invitation extended to every citizen, inviting them to participate in sculpting a city that stood as a beacon of truth, inspiring generations to come. On the horizon of NeoMind, a new dawn rose, colored by the flashes of a city that had weathered the storm and emerged stronger. At the center of this transformation was Leah, her spirit resonating with the lessons she had reaped along the way. It was a beacon in the midst of darkness, a symbol of hope in a community that, after surviving the gloom, embraced a new understanding.

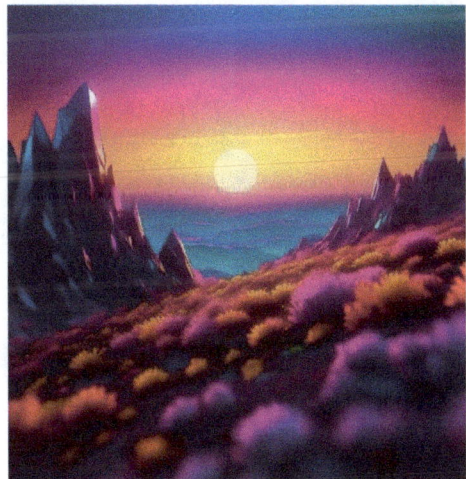

Her steps reflected the healing power of authentic memories, as she led the way to a personal redemption that illuminated the souls of those who were influenced by it.

www.ingramcontent.com/pod-product-compliance
Lightning Source LLC
Chambersburg PA
CBHW061105210326
41597CB00021B/3988